WHY YOUR LIFE Sucks

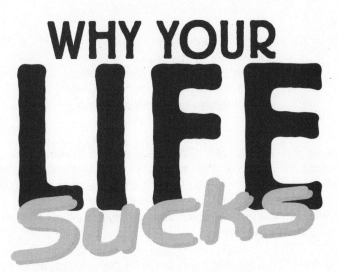

...and what you can do about it

ALAN H. COHEN

JODERE
GROUP
San Diego, California

JODERE GROUP, INC.
P.O. Box 910147
San Diego, CA 92191-0147
(800) 569-1002
www.jodere.com

Book design by Charles McStravick

The author of this book does not dispense medical advice or prescribe the use of any techniques as forms of treatment for physical or medical problems without the advice of a physician, either directly or indirectly. The intent of the author is only to offer information of a general nature to help you in your quest for emotional and spiritual well-being. In the event you use any of the information in this book for yourself, which is your constitutional right, the author and the publisher assume no responsibility for your actions.

Library of Congress Cataloging-in-Publication Data

Cohen, Alan, 1950-
    Why your life sucks : and what you can do about it / by Alan H. Cohen
      p. cm.
    ISBN 1-58872-026-8
     1. Self-actualization (Psychology) I. Title.

BF637.S4 C646 2002
158.1--dc21

                                2002072862

ISBN 1-58872-028-4

04 03 02   4 3 2
2nd printing, August 2002

Printed in the United States of America

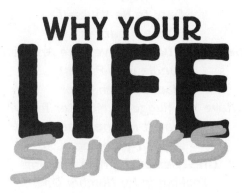

WHY YOUR
LIFE
Sucks

ALSO BY
ALAN H. COHEN

BOOKS

Are You as Happy as Your Dog?
Dare to Be Yourself
A Deep Breath of Life
The Dragon Doesn't Live Here Anymore*
Handle with Prayer*
Happily Even After
Have You Hugged a Monster Today?
I Had It All the Time*
Joy Is My Compass
Lifestyles of the Rich in Spirit
Looking in for Number One
My Father's Voice
The Peace That You Seek
Rising in Love
Setting the Seen
The Wisdom of the Heart

*Also available as Book on Tape

CASSETTE TAPES AND CDs

Deep Relaxation
Eden Morning
I Believe in You
Journey to the Center of the Heart (also CD)
Living from the Heart
Peace

VIDEO

Wisdom of the Spirit

To Abraham, Esther,
and Jerry

Who remind me
that I am already
a guest at the banquet

CONTENTS

ACKNOWLEDGMENTS

Like a wave about to crest, this book represents an ocean behind it. I am grateful to all of my teachers and friends over many years who have supported me to be who I am and do what I do.

I honor my parents, Robert and Jeane Cohen, for loving me and creating the space for me to make choices that empowered me. May my life be a blessing to your memory.

I am grateful to all of my teachers who have guided and inspired me to fan the flame of truth in my life and turn challenges into stepping stones: Mr. Simmons; Rabbi Stuart Warner; Arlene Unger; Tom Liguori; Ram Dass; Hilda Charlton; Patricia Sun; Leo Buscaglia; *A Course in Miracles*; Pat Rodegast and Emmanuel; Carla Gordan and Mary; Savizar and Solera; Jerry and Esther Hicks and Abraham, and many, many more.

This book has come to birth through the shared vision and contribution of many visionary friends. I thank Kimo O'Brien for his friendship and support over the years, and his brainstorm for this title; Michael Ebeling for his stalwart dedication and belief in this work and his tireless efforts to bring it to many recipients; Mary Traynor for taking good care of our office and all the people with whom we communicate; Debbie Luican, Beth Orvis, and the good people at the Jodere Group for their enthusiasm for this work, and their passion and skill to deliver quality material from many sources; Joel Roberts for his keen insight and inspiration to teach authentically; and Solters and Digny for their creativity in reaching those whose lives might improve through this message.

I especially thank Dee Winn for walking by my side lovingly and supportingly, selflessly empowering me to bring it forth. What a gift in such a companion!

May this book reach all those who can benefit by it, and bless everyone with tools to create a better life.

INTRODUCTION

I can still feel my hand trembling as I grasped the classroom's cold doorknob. I took a deep breath, closed my eyes, offered a silent prayer, and entered, standing as tall as I could to keep from caving in. I set my briefcase down on the teacher's desk and turned to face the class I would have given anything to avoid. I scanned their faces. Some of them already knew; they sat quite still. Others did not know yet; they were chatting amiably, some laughing. Soon their lightheartedness would give way to shock and dismay.

I took another breath and gathered all the strength I could. "Good evening," I began. They all quieted. I hesitated a moment, then forced myself to speak. "I have some very sad news to tell you." I could sense their apprehension. "Dr. Doughty will not be with us tonight . . . or again . . . he passed away over the weekend." The rest of the faces blanched. I paused and felt my jaw clench. There was no more avoiding it. Spit it out. "He took his own life."

A wave of gasps shot through the class. Then came the tears. It was done.

At the age of 22, I was the graduate teaching assistant for a college class for adults seeking to return to the work force. The course was intended to inspire them to build their self-esteem to achieve their personal and professional goals. Six weeks into the class, their professor locked himself in his garage, turned on his car engine, and asphyxiated himself. Not very inspiring. Try abysmally discouraging. Now I had to pick up the pieces, get the class back on track, and give these people some hope that their future would be brighter than their teacher's.

No one had any clue that Dr. Doughty was so unhappy. A nice-looking man in his late 30s, with a boyish grin, the professor was brilliant and charismatic. His life seemed charmed with a prestigious well-paying position, many friends, and an attractive devoted girlfriend. Yet even while Dr. Doughty had an advanced degree in psychology and taught others how to make sense of their lives, he could not find purpose in his own. In spite of all appearances, Dr. Doughty's life sucked. And it sucked to the point that he thought he had to leave it in order to find peace.

That night I quit believing in facades of happiness. It became clear to me—like a two-by-four between the eyes—that there are all kinds of things going on inside of people that we don't hear about until it is too late. That people who appear successful on the outside are often aching on the inside. That couples who smile and look great at parties often go home feeling empty and lost, and their marriages end in affairs loaded with pain and heartache. That people with great bodies or whopping bank accounts have no idea who their real friends are and go to sleep lonelier than those who are poorer and less attractive. Many people's lives suck and onlookers never know it. Many people's lives suck and *they* don't know it. Or they do, but they can't figure out how to escape the prison whose walls seem too thick to break through and too high to scale.

If your life sucks in any way; if the life you are living on the outside doesn't match who you are on the inside; or if you are hurting and feel powerless—this book offers you a road map out of hell. You can either go on putting up with your pain and die a little bit more each day as you helplessly drift from your dreams and heart's desires—or you can take the way out.

Perhaps your whole life doesn't suck. Maybe one aspect of it sucks. Maybe it's your job, or your relationship, or your money, or you just don't feel well. Or maybe things are good most of the time, and they suck some of the time. It doesn't matter. When it sucks, it sucks. Do you want to just settle for a less-than life, or would you like to get it handled?

"Sucks" used to be a dirty word, but now we hear it everywhere. You can say it on television, in school, and read it in movie reviews. The word is brilliantly descriptive! When something sucks, it saps your energy and undermines the quality of your life. It makes you feel smaller and wish you hadn't participated. It sabotages your joy and you walk away feeling crummy.

When it comes to your life sucking, you can't just walk away from it. You can't just put your life aside and go on to something else that feels better. When your life sucks, that's serious. It's a big wake-up call. It's an invitation to *do something different*. Not more of the same. If coins keep falling out of a hole in your pocket, the answer is not to go out and get a second job. The answer is to plug the hole.

This book will help you find and patch any leaks in your system. It is honest and practical, with teeth. I grew up in New Jersey, you know (Exit 9). Jersey people can get in your face if they want to. But so can life. If your life is getting in your face, you might want to know why, so you can do something about it before it gets worse. As you face and plug each hole, you will transform every challenge into a gift. Together we can turn tragedy into triumph and make it all a win.

Just a few pages from now, I'll walk you through the ten most common things you might be doing that can make your life suck. Then I'll show you how to reverse them. You are not a victim—you are a powerful creator. You can make the changes in your life that will get you the results you want. I guarantee that if you practice the principles you learn here, your life will change for the better. Plugging one leak at a time. Along the way, you might even fall in love with yourself.

One more thing: I have done all the things you read that make life suck. I am writing from my own experience. I am an expert on these points because I have messed up so many times that I figured out what not to do again. If I can save you some of the bleeding-chin learning curve, that would make us both happy. I am simply passing along to you some of the sewing techniques that keep stuff from falling out of my pockets.

The process doesn't have to be hard. We're going to enjoy the journey. We'll laugh as we go. As you unravel the "nots" in your life and reduce the size of your "but," you will experience a new sense of freedom and exhilaration. The only thing harder than waking up is staying asleep in a nightmare. Let's do it. It's time.

YOU GIVE YOUR POWER Away

Before baseball star Mickey Mantle died, he faced and came to terms with his lifelong alcoholism. As he was withering of liver disease, Mickey held a press conference at the Betty Ford Center. A reporter asked him, "How would you like people to remember Mickey Mantle?" Pale and gaunt, still sporting his Yankee cap, he replied, "I would like them to think that I finally made something of myself." I was shocked. One of the most loved and celebrated sports heroes of all time—my hero—did not respect himself until he took back the power he had given to his addiction.

A few months later, Mickey Mantle died. Soon afterward I saw a touching newspaper cartoon showing Mickey meeting God, depicted as a person. As the two ambled down a long road in heaven, God placed his arm around Mickey's shoulder. Mickey turned to God and wistfully remarked, "I can't believe all the errors I made." God turned to Mickey and answered, "But you gave them a ninth inning they'll never forget."

We have all given our power away to something—many things—and our lives have sucked for it. We have bestowed undue power to lovers, money, bosses, addictive substances, fame, dream homes, religious dogma, parents, children, doctors, lawyers, agents, therapists, psychics, teachers, policemen, politicians, sports heroes, movie stars, gorgeous men and women, business moguls, the news, and occult sciences. The list goes on; you can add more of your own.

> *You give your power away when you*
> *make someone or something outside of you*
> *more important than what is inside of you.*

If you do not value who and what you are, you will seek to borrow worth from the outer world. You will look for validation from people whom you believe know or have more than you. But since everything you need is inside you and no one can know more about your path and purpose than you do, any power you ascribe to external authorities must eventually explode in your face and leave you feeling worse than when you started. The question is not, "Have you given your power away?" The question is, "How can you get it back?"

Unsucking your life is an inside job. You do not need to import power, for you were born with it; you just need to plug the holes in your bucket through which it is leaking. The quest is about peeling away the lies and illusions you have been told—and went on to tell yourself—that have kept you living smaller than you deserve. When you do, you will be amazed to realize how much you have settled for. Then you will have little patience for halfhearted living and reclaim your right to live from choice rather than default.

Any experience that leaves you feeling empty, less-than, or needy does so for only one reason: You entered into it feeling empty, less-than, or needy. The illusion is that relationships will take away the pain that keeps you feeling small; the reality is that relationships *magnify* the pain that keeps you feeling small. And yet there is a gift in the process: you remember that *the source of your strength is inside you.*

Perhaps the final lines of Woody Allen's classic movie *Annie Hall* sum up how we stay trapped in painful situations: A man says to a psychiatrist, "My wife thinks she's a chicken and she's driving me crazy!" The psychiatrist asks him, "So why don't you leave her?" The man answers, "I can't— I need the eggs."

You don't need the eggs anymore. They are rotten, taste horrible, and don't nourish you. When you elevate others at your expense, nobody wins. When you source your life from inside out, everyone wins. As you strike gold in your own self, you will quit giving the people in your world a carbon copy of the terror that runs their lives, and give them a ninth inning— or a first, or a fifth—they'll never forget.

How You Give Your Power Away and What You Can Do

You Put People on a Pedestal

Former child movie star, Shirley Temple Black discovered a flaw in the pedestal game at a young age. She recounts, *"I stopped believing in Santa Claus when I was six. Mother took me to see him in a department store and he asked for my autograph."* The savior she sought was also seeking a savior in her.

Idols always fall on those who worship them. The bigger the idol, the harder it crashes. If you think any person has the power, wealth, wisdom, beauty, talent, or strength to rescue you from your deficits, you set yourself up for trouble. Yes, there are people who can help, support, and teach you. No, there is no one out there who can save you. That is something you have to do yourself by recognizing you already own what you seek.

When you have a crush on someone, you will be crushed. That's why they call it a crush. You crush reality out of the other person by seeing them through the eyes of fantasy, while you crush your own self-worth. Face it: crushes buy you a ticket to a wild emotional roller coaster ride. For every giddy rush you experience, you will soon be plummeting. Mr. Right smiles at you and you are in heaven; the next day he looks the other way and you are in hell. And you call this *a relationship?* You wrap your soul in a little package, hand it to someone you don't even know, and instruct them, "Here, do with this as you wish."

Crushes stay in force only from a distance. It is easy to make a god out of a movie star, rock idol, sports hero, girl in the class above you, executive across the hall, someone else's spouse, or amorphous cyberspace fantasy lover. But if you spent time on a daily basis with your idol you would discover they are a real person, just like you. You would find things you like about them and things you don't like. He compares you to his former lovers and picks his toenails at the kitchen table. She has morning breath and unresolved father issues. In a short time your fantasy lover crashes from Mt. Olympus to Brooklyn. Ah, now you can have a real relationship, built from the earth up instead of heaven down. And along the way you will discover your own worth, intrinsic in you rather than bestowed by them.

If you indulge someone else putting you on a pedestal, be prepared for an insurrection. When they discover you are not who they thought you were or they cannot have you, out come the spears. It takes just a six-inch fall for a halo to become a noose. Rock star Selena was killed by the former president of her fan club. To avoid such an untimely demise, stand naked in your humanity and refuse to accept goo-goo-eyed adoration, which always comes with a price tag.

In the course of my work I have occasionally received letters from women who believe I am their soul mate. While I feel complimented, there is one problem in the equation: they don't really know me. They read my book or attended my seminar, and decided I am the one for them. (Yes, I have done the same kind of thing.) When this first happened, I didn't know how to handle their expression of affection and gave them ambiguous responses or none. But my non-plan backfired. Sooner or later I would receive an angry letter chastising me for letting them down and not being the person I claimed to be. But I never claimed to be that person. They claimed I was that person, and were upended by their lofty expectations. Then six months later I would receive another letter saying, "Please forgive me. I was insane." Now I am very careful not to put others on a pedestal or encourage anyone to do the same to me. I respond as one perfectly imperfect human being to another, which honors them along with me, and paves the way for true communication. Plato explained, "True friendship can occur only among equals."

Cults are an extreme example of giving power away to a spiritual leader. Rather than projecting romantic fantasies, followers project religious fantasies. But the dynamics are the same; self-effacement always leads to anger, depression, and self-strangling. Religious leaders with integrity do not accept such adoration, but deflect their followers' desire to idolize. They demonstrate by example there is just as much God in the student as the teacher. Buddhists teach, "If you meet the Buddha on the road, kill him." If you encounter someone whom you believe embodies more divinity than you, get rid of the notion immediately. We are all equal expressions of the Great Spirit, and you only hurt yourself by elevating someone above you. Why become a Buddhist when you can become a Buddha? Carl Jung exclaimed, "Thank God I am not a Jungian." I wonder if Jesus might say something similar. The cult mentality leads to aberrant behavior like mass suicides at Jonestown and Heaven's Gate. Bottom line: If someone tells you what tennis shoes to wear, run like hell.

It's going to be tricky falling in love with yourself if you are fascinated with someone else. You can love someone, respect them, learn from them, have a fabulous time with them, and honor them as a role model. Just don't diminish yourself in the process. We are told that Jesus said, "Even greater things than I, shall you do," indicating he regarded his students as powerful in their own right. Recognize that power within you, and you won't have any pedestals crashing on you. Don't just love the one you're with—be the one you love.

You Imitate Instead of Create

Imitation is the sincerest form of flattery, but self-suffocating if you do not grow beyond it. Ralph Waldo Emerson declared, "Imitation is suicide." To those who do not recognize their unique worth, imitations looms attractive; to those who know their strength, imitation represents an unacceptable compromise.

In the early stages of skill or character development, imitation is helpful if you choose a good role model. When I first learned to cook, I used recipes and turned out some tasty dishes. But after a while I grew bored. Why follow someone else's formula when I could create my own? After that, I never cooked the same dish twice. Cooking became a great adventure! Imitating role models is like using training wheels on a child's bicycle; they help you get going, but once you find your own rhythm and balance, you fly faster and farther without leaning on them.

In relationships, imitation can hurt us if we subconsciously hold poor role models. If, as a child, you observed people whose lives sucked, you may have accepted their fear and pain as normal and gone on to settle for what they did. Then you espouse your culture's prejudices, recreate your parents' marriage, and become the parent your parents were to you. If you were empowered by the models you observed, you are good to go. But if what you saw delivered heartache, you cannot afford to perpetuate it. If you do not make strong choices for yourself, you will reap the results of the weak choices of others.

In the field of entertainment, our culture glorifies celebrities who are talented in one domain but have not come to terms with the deeper issues of their lives. They look great on screen, run like lightning on the football field, or boast impressive bottom lines on their financial statements—but when they step off screen or the playing field, their personal lives are disastrous. Then you read about them O.D.'ing, shooting someone, or mucking through a colossal divorce battle. They are great role models for talent, but terrible models for character. If you are going to emulate someone, focus on their talent, not their aberration. Or just pick someone who is happy.

Imitation also backfires on us in education. As sophisticated as our school system is, it still rewards conformity far more than originality. If you learn how to play the school game, you can regurgitate your way through your doctorate and still live a million miles from joy. Many of my college psychology professors were neurotic, confused, and caught up in a gnarly rat race of performance, competition, and mind games. Meanwhile, the custodian who cleaned their offices whistled, smiled, and had a kind word for everyone he met. Who was closer to winning the game of life?

In many industries you can maintain a livelihood by executing the formula. Mass-market movies have a formula, as do novels and marketing plans. They work, and they work for a reason. But such creations are typically nonmemorable and do not make any significant contribution except to put money in the pockets of the producers. Blessed is the person who is willing to follow their gut impulse to create something unique, beyond the known. Think of the movies, books, teachers, and friends who have affected you most deeply, and you will realize that they did not fit the mold. They touched you because their creations were motivated by inspiration, not desperation. The world is changed not by those who do what has been done before them, but by those who do what has been done inside them.

*Creativity is as much a
muscle as the heart,
and no less vital.*

The more creative you are, the more creative you become; deny your visions, and they atrophy. Creative people are tapped into an endless resource of ideas. A creator's dilemma is not running out of material; it is what to do with all the material knocking at the door of imagination. (Bumper sticker: *Reality is for people who can't deal with imagination.*) You will not connect with your muse by following the herd; most of them are rambling over a cliff. A smaller flock will take off when they reach the edge. If you have been hypnotized to believe you are a lemming, you will plunge with the crowd. If you remember you have wings, you will soar.

*Fortune is not something that happens to you.
It is something you create.*

You can make anything work in your favor. Study your role models, accept the gifts they have bestowed, and leave behind what does not serve you. Then you can say, like Gary de Rodriguez, "I stand on the shoulders of my ancestors' tragedies and declare triumph, and know that they are cheering me on."

You Don't Listen to Your Intuition

Goethe proclaimed, "When you finally trust yourself, you will know how to live." If you look back on mistakes you have made, you can usually identify a little voice inside your head that was nudging you otherwise. "I can't believe I overlooked all the red flags," you may note. We get into trouble not because we do not know what to do, but because we do not pay attention to what we know.

While you might regret not heeding your inner voice, the experience leaves you with an important lesson:

You have access to impeccable wisdom all the time.

Imagine a radio station that we'll call K-N-O-W broadcasting—sound advice from somewhere deep inside you 24 hours a day. Then imagine you have a tuner capable of receiving its signal. If you set your tuner to the right frequency, you hear the broadcast and pick up vital information. If your dial is set elsewhere, you miss the message.

You were born with your tuner set to KNOW. Children and animals have their tuners well set; they know who they are and can sense people and situations that match their well-being or threaten it. As you became socialized, you were seduced away from KNOW. You were taught that you are selfish if you do what you really want to do; wrong if you disobey your parents' wish for the kind of mate they would choose for you; or foolish if you pursued a career in the arts that did not net an income as lucrative as computer programming. Eventually externally-generated signals drowned out the voice of KNOW, and you felt lost and confused. But you are not stupid; you just disregarded what you knew in deference to the outer voices shrieking at you.

Ignorance and errors are easily rectified by respecting your inner genius. Several years ago I was planning to meet my musician friend Charley Thweatt in Los Angeles for a seminar we were to co-present. Charley's flight was scheduled to arrive at 10 A.M., but in order for me to arrive around that time I would have had to fly out of Portland around 6 A.M. Although I could have done this, something inside me told me to book a later flight. I judged myself as being lazy and felt guilty for asking Charley to wait hours for me, but I decided to go with my gut and I booked a flight to land around 2 P.M. When I arrived, Charley was not there. I phoned his airline and learned that his connecting flight through Denver had been delayed by snow. He finally arrived at 3 P.M. Listening to my inner voice paid off big time.

Your gut knowing is keenly aware of your right place and it signals you when you approach unhealthy situations. Animals become restless when an earthquake is imminent; studies show a correlation between newspaper ads for lost pets and earthquakes that soon follow. Other studies indicate a higher rate of last-minute cancellations for airplane flights that crash. While we may be tempted to look outside ourselves for advice, we are all quite brilliant and know a lot more about our path and destiny than we recognize.

When something is right for you, something inside you knows. I once did a fascinating radio interview with a host who posed the question to callers, "How do you recognize when something is true or good for you?" The switchboard lit up with calls from many people eager to describe their unique way of knowing. Some people reported feeling warmth around their heart; others told that the hairs on the back of their neck stood up; some described a feeling like a cool breeze on their cheeks and arms, or simply a sense of peace, ease, and relief, as if to say, "Yes, this path really matches me." One caller recounted that when she was taking a multiple-choice test, the correct answers seemed to "light up" with extra energy; she ended up with the highest score in the class!

For thousands of years, people seeking guidance have consulted an oracle. Yet they could have received impeccable advice by consulting the auricle—the chamber of their own heart. In ancient Egypt when someone died, attendants saved the person's heart, which they believed to be the seat of true wisdom. We have been trained to go to only our brain for answers, while the heart offers deeper wisdom. Successful leaders make use of both faculties. When General Colin Powell was being drafted to run for President in the early stages of the 2000 race, he declined, noting, "What wasn't pulling me was my inner compass and my sense of who I am."

Your intuition is especially good at timing. You don't need a watch as much as you need KNOW. On many occasions I have had to wake up at a particular time, but did not have an alarm clock. My inner timekeeper took over and responded impeccably. One morning I had to wake up at 7 o'clock. As I opened my eyes, the second hand on the clock was touching the number 12 at precisely 7 A.M.!

I once took a kayak out with a friend and paddled up the Hanalei River on the magnificent island of Kauai. When we rented the kayak in the morning, I left my wallet and car keys at the rental office for safekeeping. Later in the day, far upstream, we pulled the kayak off to the side of the river and rested in the high grasses. Suddenly it occurred to me that I did not know when the rental office would close and we might need to get back by a certain time to retrieve my valuables. I put the idea off, but a minute later I felt a very strong urge to leave, as if someone was prodding me with a poker. I interrupted our conversation in mid-sentence and said, "Let's go back now." We paddled back gracefully and arrived at precisely 5 P.M.—just as the manager was locking the door for the night. Talk about timing!

But there's more: Standing with the manager were two of my friends from Maui, seeking to rent a kayak. The manager was explaining to them that it was too late. But our kayak still had the remainder of a 24-hour rental. So we gave them our kayak and they got a free trip!

This experience demonstrates that intuition operates at a level far deeper than the surface mind. I did not know what time the kayak office closed; we had no timepiece; and I certainly had no idea my friends would be at the office seeking a rental. When you trust your inner promptings and act on them, synchronicity works with amazing precision.

If you had access to an advisor who gave you perfect guidance every time you consulted them, would you not go there first? Such an advisor exists, and you have entrée now. Just pay more attention to what is going on inside you than what is going on around you. Don't wait until you are bruised and beaten from ramming into dead ends to which you are led by voices other than your own. Move from your deepest knowing, and all the right doors will open.

*Drop what you've been taught
so you can remember what you know.*

You Let Others Choose for You

In the brilliant movie, *The Truman Show,* Jim Carrey portrays a man who, unbeknownst to him, lives his entire life on a bigger-than-life television set. While Truman thinks he is making free personal choices, every aspect of his life is manipulated by a calculating producer watching from a distant control booth. Eventually Truman gets wind of the scheme and tries to escape from the small town he has never ventured beyond. But in order to keep their popular television show alive, the producers stage obstacle after obstacle against Truman's attempts to break free. At one point, an assistant in the control booth asks the producer, "Do you think he will be able to find his way out?" The producer soberly answers, "If he was absolutely determined to leave, he could at anytime. The truth is that he prefers his world."

Is the life you are living one that you prefer, or one that others prefer for you? Sometimes it seems easier to let other people decide for you, and in matters that are inconsequential, it is no big deal. But if you make important life choices by default, you will never know who you are or deliver your unique gifts to the world. Some people would rather do anything than rock the boat—even if it were sinking.

Benjamin Franklin noted, "Most people die at age 25, but they are not buried until 75." Physical death is mandatory, but spiritual death is optional. And tragic. You can be walking through normal activities, by all appearances fully alive, but if your soul is decrepit, you cannot truly say you are living.

How much life you embody or miss depends on how true you are to your personal choices. Robert Louis Stevenson noted, *"To know what you prefer instead of humbly saying 'Amen' to what the world tells that you ought to prefer, is to have kept your soul alive."*

I saw a fascinating television investigative news story about the use of public telephones. When callers dial a long-distance number from a pay phone, an operator comes on the line and asks them which long-distance company they want to use. If the caller does not have one in mind, they say something like, "I don't care," or "Whatever." In response, some calculating entrepreneurs have established phone companies with names like "The Whatever Phone Company" or "Doesn't Matter Communications." When the operator hears, "Doesn't Matter," she routes the call through that company's billing system. Then the caller receives a huge bill, like $9 for directory assistance. This is all perfectly legal. It works because people leave their choices to others.

If you don't use your mind,
someone else will.

In junior high school Dave Barry was a class clown and often found himself in trouble for cracking jokes during class. One day his teacher scolded him, "You'd better get to work, Dave Barry. You can't joke your way through life, you know."

Fortunately, Dave paid no attention to his teacher and went on to become the most successful humor writer in America. With many popular books to his credit, he writes the most widely syndicated humor column in American newspapers. And won a Pulitzer Prize along the way.

Dave Barry *is* joking his way through life, and doing quite well at it. If he had buckled under his teacher's pressure and done something that was safe but boring, millions of us would have missed out on some precious insights and belly laughs. And he would have been just one more walking corpse.

Take care each day that you are more than a zombie and your long distance carrier doesn't grab you by the calls. In the long run, you are the one who will have to live with your decisions, so make sure they represent your true desires.

You Think Your Destiny Depends on Something Outside You

When you are not aware that your best source of answers is *you*, you go looking elsewhere. We are like the musk deer, who searches the mountains and valleys for the source of an intoxicating aroma, only to discover it was emanating from its own self. Buddha asked, *"If you do not get it from yourself, where will you go for it?"*

On an episode of the television show *Northern Exposure*, a young woman named Shelly receives a chain letter promising that if she mails the letter to a friend within three days, good luck will come to her. She decides to give it a try and mails her letter at the local grocery store/post office in her little town. Immediately Shelly begins to receive money, meet men, and enjoy all manner of success she has been seeking for a long time. She is ecstatic—the letter really worked! A week later Shelly returns to the post office, where the clerk holds up her unmailed letter and informs her, "I've been waiting for you to come back; your letter needed more postage." Stunned, Shelly realizes the chain letter did not create her run of luck—she did. She concludes, *"I guess I'm in charge of my own life after all."*

So are we all. Your life is not what the stars, numbers, genetics, environment, politics, or economic conditions make it; it is what you make it. External variables influence, but internal variables determine.

To really live, let go of any idea
that anything outside you
determines your destiny.
The force that determines
your destiny is you.

Dump the concept of luck. Lucky people attract positive events because they think lucky. People who continually attract negative events hold patterns of thought that match them. *What you dwell on, you dwell in.* Your stars and numbers do not cause; they reflect. In the long run, they are what you make of them. Any divination system is only as good as it honors your power to choose. Even the best psychics acknowledge that nothing is set in stone. Events may be headed in a direction, but free will always supercedes predestination. Remove the "pre" from predestination, and you get to choose your own destination. If an advisor, including a physician, tells you that you are stuck with a certain situation for life and have no control over it, run even faster than from the people who tell you what tennis shoes to wear. You have just fallen into power denial. You have access to greater possibilities.

You can create a thriving personal economy in the midst of recession; stay vitally healthy in the midst of "the flu going around"; find a delicious mate in the midst of a field of total Bozos; develop a career that you love *and* pays you money; change your life path at any age; create a relationship that includes intimacy *and* freedom; take as many vacations as you choose; do your laundry naked; do nothing and be totally worthwhile; have wild sex *and* be totally spiritual; love and respect yourself even if someone else doesn't; watch your kids grow up to be happy, creative adults in spite of their pierced tongues and buttock tattoos; find a blessing in experiences you once felt guilty about; and have your body function well until the day you *decide* to leave.

If any or all of this sounds like too much to ask, you still think someone or something outside you pulls the strings of your life. But anything less than living fully from choice is too *little* to ask. Your true strength resides in holding your power in the midst of those who have abdicated theirs. Most people take what is given them and assume it is their destiny. Great spirits take what is given them and make their own destiny.

Take what you have
and make what you want.

When you are ready to stand in your own authority, your world will reshape itself around your intentions. The words authority and authentic derive from the same root word, which signifies that the route to genuine power is realness. Real power is not power over others; it is power to be yourself. Anyone who needs to dominate or defeat others to feel powerful is disconnected from their authentic power. When you struggle with another for power, neither of you have it. Any power you vie for is not worth having; while someone seems to win, both lose. As Lily Tomlin noted, "The trouble with the rat race is that even if you win, you're still a rat." Real power does not compete; it finds a way to synchronize. It is not a limited commodity someone can take from you; it is unlimited energy available to everyone at all times. If everyone lived from their true power, we would take the energy we have invested in strife and reallocate it for unprecedented achievement.

No matter how much you have given your power away, the game is not over until you reclaim it. This is not a game of sudden death, but sudden life. It appears that people live until they die, while in reality they die until they live. No matter how long you have traveled; what trials you have faced; and what errors you have made, you can transform it all into gold. Everything you have gone through is a setup for awakening. You don't need to wait until you die for God to remind you how great you are. Remind yourself now, and you will play the game of your life.

YOU EXPECT IT TO
Suck

At sunset on a pleasant July evening, eight-year-old Jesse Arbogast was playing in murky waters close to Gulf Islands National Seashore in Florida. Behind him, a seven-foot bull shark silently stalked. Suddenly, Jesse felt a shocking wrench on his right arm, followed by excruciating pain. In one terrible moment, his arm was gone.

Jesse's uncle Vance watched the grisly scene from the beach and plunged into the bloody waters. He grabbed the shark by the tail, freed Jesse, and wrestled the shark to shore. A park ranger arrived, fired three bullets to subdue the beast, and then reached into the shark's mouth to retrieve Jesse's severed arm. Within 20 minutes Jesse was airlifted to a hospital, where he arrived with no breath, pulse, or blood pressure. A team of doctors worked 11 hours through the night to reattach Jesse's arm. The operation was successful and Jesse regained consciousness. Today he has use of both arms.

This extraordinary account demonstrates our power to choose rather than settle. When faced with the awful scenario Jesse's uncle encountered, most people would have simply watched horrified and called for help. A few would have snatched the boy from the sea and hoped he lived. But that was not good enough for Uncle Vance. He wanted his nephew alive, and he wanted both of his arms intact. And that is what he got.

If you settle for less than what you really want, you will get exactly that. If you expect your life to suck, it will. Many of us have spent a lot of our lives trying to swim through life missing an arm. Painful experiences have gnawed away our resilience and chewed up our initiative. Some of us have swum one-armed for so long (and observed so many others doing so) that we have come to accept brokenness as a fact of life and do not question swimming in circles. But you don't need to continue. If you refuse to settle for dismembered existence, you can restore your wholeness. Your arm is not lost; it's just been snatched and hidden. Like Jesse, you may need help from a benevolent, courageous uncle—but be assured the support you need is available. You do not walk alone.

How You Expect Your Life to Suck and What You Can Do

You Accept Phony Limits from Others without Questioning

When I was a little boy, my mother told me never to flush the toilet while I was sitting on it, or else I would get a "cold in the tush." Since my mother knew everything, I believed her. For many years I avoided flushing while sitting, confident I was escaping the dreaded tush cold.

Then one day at the age of about 30, I was sitting on the toilet and I inadvertently reached to flush. The moment my fingers touched the cold steel, I was overtaken by terror—I almost accidentally summoned the awful tush monster from his fathomless lair!

But then, for the first time in my life, I called this belief into question. Would I *really* get a cold in my tush if I flushed prematurely? And what is a tush cold, anyway?

I had to find out for myself. I pressed down on the lever and took my chances. Once and for all I would find out how vulnerable my tush actually was. But nothing happened. No tush cold. Not even a sniffle. I was liberated!

This experience, silly as it might sound, stands quite symbolic. As children we were taught many erroneous, limiting, and debilitating beliefs. We were told what boys and girls each could and couldn't do; which color of people were acceptable and which to avoid; how much money and stuff you had to have to be respectable; how long people in your family live and what they die of; what are your chances of surviving cancer; and what you would surely go to hell for. Our innocent little minds were crammed with judgments, fears, statistics, and expectations that, like the bull shark, cut off our reach and ripped our self-respect to shreds. Then, without testing these limits, we went on to live as if they were true.

I know a fellow who, as a young boy, heard his father tell him time and again, "You'll be the death of me!" Then, when his father died suddenly of a heart attack, he plunged into deep guilt as if his father's death was his fault. Another man struggled for many years with guilt about sex. Then, as an adult, he observed his mother baby-sitting a two-year-old boy. When she saw the child fondling his penis, she sharply reprimanded him, "Don't you dare touch your penis—it is for urinating only!" Instantly the man realized how he had learned to feel guilty about sex. His guilt was not innate, but learned. And what is learned can be unlearned.

A woman named Rita underwent minor surgery for some reproductive system problems. After the surgery, to everyone's surprise, she was not recovering. Tests revealed there was nothing physically wrong with her. To try to get to the root of her problem, a psychologist was called in. He hypnotized Rita and discovered that while she was under anesthesia, she had heard her doctor say, "There is no way she is going to survive more than a day or two." The psychologist asked the surgeon if he had made this statement, and he admitted he had—but it was in response to a question he was asked about another patient! Although Rita was under anesthesia, her subconscious registered the thought as if it applied to her, and her body played it out. (Rita continued to work with the psychologist and eventually recovered.)

We have all been hypnotized into thinking that we are smaller than we are. Just as an undersized flower pot keeps a mighty tree root-bound or a little fishbowl keeps goldfish tiny, we have adapted, adjusted, and accommodated to a Lilliputian life. But place the same tree in an open field or the fish in a lake, and they will grow to hundreds of times their size. Unlike the tree or goldfish, you are not dependent on someone else to move you. You have the power to move yourself. You can step into a broader domain and grow to your full potential.

Do not limit life to your beliefs.
Expand your beliefs to encompass
all that life has to offer.

Should you feel tempted to rail against your parents, perpetrator, priest, or police for screwing you up, don't waste your energy. You are misappropriating the power you could be using to reattach your arm. Your enemies are not the people who impressed you with illusions; they suffered under the same hypnosis, and need compassion rather than blame. Rebecca McClen Novick explained, "We are protagonists and the authors of our own drama. It is up to us; there is no one left to blame. Neither the system, nor our leaders, nor our parents. We can't go out and hang the first amoeba."

Your real enemies are the self-defeating thoughts, paltry expectations, and beliefs that you must live at less than full throttle. You will experience as much pain as you are willing to accept. You *do* have control over how much you hurt. Pain happens; suffering is optional. You can choose thoughts that bring you relief rather than imprisonment. To find your freedom, stand at the doorway of your mind and monitor your thoughts. Notice which ones lift you and which ones drag you down. Then, like a bouncer at an exclusive party, admit only those on the invitation list and send the others back where they came from. Fate is not a net cast over you by capricious fortune; it is a garden you cultivate by the thoughts you attend to. Shift your attention and you will shift your life.

The only way to find out if the limits under which you have been living are real is to test them. A healthy belief will stand in the face of challenge. Illusions will evaporate. If you do not test your beliefs, they will become your ruler and you their hostage. When you hold your identity as "less-than" up to the light, it will fade into nothingness. It owned you only because you never questioned it. You are bigger than any difficulty that could confront you. Grab it by the tail and you immobilize it. Your moment of upset is your opportunity to reprogram and choose anew.

To be a master, act like one. Assuming greatness is not phony; unworthiness is the imposter. You may have played small for a long time and fallen prey to the hallucination, "I can't." But behind every "can't" is a "won't." When you reach the chalk circle others have drawn around you, keep walking. The moment you look a monster in the eye and demand, "Show me what you really are," the beast will shapeshift into an ally. Emerson proclaimed, "Do the thing you fear, and the death of fear is certain." When dark and light are placed in the same room, light always wins. And because your nature is light, you will triumph over every limit you have learned.

You Believe You Deserve Pain

If you harbor any belief you are guilty, sinful, or evil, or that punishment pays off a debt you have incurred, you will just keep suffering. Ongoing pain arrives not by the hand of a wrathful God exacting vengeance; it is a statement of your ability to manufacture a reality and live in it.

If you have borne a weighty cross of guilt, you can drop it now. The source of your problems is not a ruthless universe; it is your fearful mind. You can renew your mind and life by choosing thoughts that honor your worth and deliver you from execution to exultation. What you created at will, you can dis-create at will. In several rarely acknowledged or quoted Bible verses we are told, "You are gods, sons of the Most High, all of you." We are gods in the sense that God has given us the power of choice to create our life. Guilt and the entire world it engenders represent a choice, and so do innocence and the gifts it bears.

We have learned many unfounded justifications for punishment. They all appear to be delivered from the outside world, while they are really self-inflicted. Original Sin, for one, supposes you are guilty just for being born. Someone who came before you did something terrible, and you are accountable for it. Simply because you live and breathe, you are deficient and you owe. If you hold this concept up to the light of reason, it defies the many Bible verses that affirm we are created in the image and likeness of God. But if someone drummed guilt into you as a child, it can seem very real. You can even build a whole life on it.

Think for a moment: What kind of mind would come up with such an idea? Who could look upon a radiant newborn child, innocent and pure, a miracle in every way, and claim she or he has blood on her or his hands? I will tell you how guilt got started and how it is perpetuated: Long, long ago in a galaxy very much like this one, someone discovered that if you can get someone to feel guilty, you can control them.

A mind that adopts guilt becomes vulnerable, disempowered, and easily led. People who believe they owe a debt to a power stronger than themselves will do just about anything to placate that power and keep it at bay. Since the first guilt trip was laid and accepted, innumerable parents, husbands, wives, children, bosses, governments, cults, and middle school teachers have learned how to make others feel guilty so they can control them. But this has nothing to do with Original Sin, and everything to do with Original Dysfunction. Some religions have mastered guilt to a finely-tuned science. Guilty people will pay lots of money to have their sins removed, stay in the grace of God, and avoid hell. What they don't realize as they are writing checks to buy off Big Brother is that there is no hell worse than believing that an external force has power over you and can take away your good.

Religions, well-intentioned as they are, with many good people involved in them, can become hooked on money and power. If parishioners woke up one morning and suddenly realized that God lives within them and loves them just as they are, will they still show up on Sunday? If they didn't fear going to hell after they die, will they still marry within the faith? And how will we fund the building campaign? And so on. Is this starting to make sense?

In relationships, the primary motivator for manipulation is emotional insecurity. If I can get you to feel guilty, you will stay where I want you and do what I like. You will have sex with me, give me money, keep a roof over my head, or drive the kids where I tell you. If you feel bad enough about yourself, I will hold the power to make choices for you that serve me. We call this "love." Or "marriage." Yet love and marriage have nothing to do with keeping each other small; their purpose is to bestow richer life, not imprisonment. *It's not love if it hurts.*

A clever twist on inherited debt is guilt carried over from a past life. In this case, the person who came before you and rendered you guilty at birth is *you*. In some previous incarnation you committed some heinous act, and the chronic back pain that plagues you now is your retribution for it. *Puh-leez!* I have to confess I bought that one. Many years ago I was offered a position as a supervisor in a sheltered workshop for developmentally disabled adults, in those days labeled "severely and profoundly retarded." I wasn't particularly interested in this career, but I needed the money. I found the job depressing and overwhelming and I wanted to leave, but I felt too guilty; I couldn't bear to let these poor retarded people down. And besides, I didn't want to be a quitter. I reasoned—now don't laugh too hard—that in some past life I had been retarded and some kind bloke took care of me. Now, to offset my karmic debt, I had to spend my life caring for these unfortunate folks. In spite of this romantic notion (with a sick twist), it didn't work. After a month I became physically ill. But then I needed to stay in the job for 60 days to be eligible for the medical benefits to fund the treatments for the illness I got from being there in the first place. See how the spiral goes? I forced myself to stay, but I just felt worse and worse.

Then one day I realized that the retarded people were having more fun than I was. They arrived at the workshop each morning laughing, playing, feeling each other up, and having animated conversations with the front door. Every day at lunchtime I would take out my funky old guitar and sing a few rousing verses of "I've Been Working on the Railroad." The crowd would go wild—you'd think they had front row seats at a Michael Jackson concert! Meanwhile I just kept dragging myself through the day like the corpse in *Weekend at Bernie's*. After a few weeks I no longer felt sorry for the retarded people. I envied them.

Eventually I became so dispirited that I overcame my fear of God punishing me for leaving; after all, I was dying right where I was, and I had nothing to lose. So I mustered the courage to give notice. The moment I spoke the words to my supervisor, my life force returned. Within a short time my symptoms disappeared and I got back on track with my joy. That is when I began to write, present seminars, and perform music—all of which paved the way for a most fulfilling career.

A few months after I quit, I went back to visit the sheltered workshop. There I discovered that the fellow who was hired to replace me was doing a far, far better job than I ever did. He loved being there and had a gifted manner with the clients. It was then that I realized that out of my guilt, I had been stealing that man's right job from him, and the right supervisor for those people! They were dancing while I was dragging. They had no concept they owed a karmic debt; Original Sin was as foreign to them as Keynesian Economics. I was supposed to be their guide, but they were better guides to me. They were supposed to be retarded, but in many ways they were advanced. Their child-like sense of delight advanced them, and my sense of guilt retarded me. So much for guilt.

How do you get over guilt? Here are some practical suggestions:

Reframe in Your Favor

Whenever you do something for which you are tempted to blame yourself, find a way to view it that defines you as innocent. Ask yourself how you would see such an act if it was done by someone you loved. Since you can make anything out of anything, why not interpret the event in your favor?

While visiting the home of some friends, I went into their kitchen to boil some water for tea. When I returned to their living room, we smelled something burning. We dashed into the kitchen and saw that the plastic handle of the pot was on fire—I had left it too close to the flame on the stove. I felt quite embarrassed and blew out the flame. I sheepishly looked at my host and apologized. To my surprise, he did not chastise me. Instead, he exclaimed, "My goodness, Alan, I didn't know you were such a good fireman!"

Don't Lay Guilt

"As you judge, so shall you be judged." Not by a wrathful God, but your own mind. This aphorism is not a moral indictment; it is a psychological principle: You see yourself through the same eyes as you see others, and you automatically apply to yourself the criticism or forgiveness you show them. You will also expect to be treated in the same way you treat them. When you hold another person in judgment, you hold yourself there too, as if you were keeping someone in prison and sitting at the door of their cell to make sure they don't escape. In order to stand guard, you have to stay in prison with them. Find ways to let others out of jail, and you will escape with them.

Don't Pursue Punishment

Bible adherents quote the phrase, "Vengeance is mine, thus saith the Lord." What this actually means is, "Don't get into the vengeance business." Leave it to the universe. If someone needs to learn a lesson due to their errors, it's not up to you to administer it. You gain nothing by making someone else suffer; to the contrary, you lose your own peace, which is tragic. Your forgiveness is your gift to yourself. Forgive not because the other person deserves it, but because you do. They may be wrong, evil, and the stupidest, most despicable creature to ever walk the earth. So what? The moment you spew hatred, the venom poisons your own soul. Don't waste a moment of precious life stewing over someone else; their sins are not worth it, and you are worth more. If you want to live free of punishment, don't dish it out.

Cultivate Appreciation

Each day spend a few minutes reinforcing a positive vision of yourself and your life. Use creative visualization, prayer, meditation, journaling, affirmation, or conscious intention to enhance your relationship with yourself and significant others. Use positive self-talk to affirm your wholeness, innocence, lovability, and worthiness to achieve your goals. Write down why you want the things dear to you, and why you deserve them. *Never apologize, diminish, or put yourself down* in conversations with others or your own mind. Accept compliments without deflecting them or making excuses. Become a force for your worthiness, and worthiness will become a force for you.

Act as If

When offered the opportunity to do something you desire, move ahead as if you can and will have it. If someone believes in you more than you believe in yourself, accept their belief rather than your own. Don't argue for your limits or justify your inadequacies by citing examples of past failures. You can either be right about what's wrong with you, or get what you want. Which would you rather have?

You might argue that "acting as if" is phony or unnatural. To the contrary, acting as if you are inadequate is the lie. Your phoniness lies in assuming the identity that has been laid over you by people who accepted phony identities for themselves and seek to keep you small with them. Break the spell by assuming mastery, and watch your world change.

You Believe Struggle Is Required

If you think struggle is a prerequisite for success, success will cost you big time. You have heard "no pain, no gain," for so long that you may feel guilty if something good comes to you without sweating for it. (My motto is, "no pain, no pain.") "No pain, no gain" is a half-truth. We learn just as much—often more—from joy and delight. Pain offers us the important message, "This can't be it." Joy offers us the important message: "This *is* it."

A brief anatomy lesson is in order here. You do not have one brain, but two. Your primal brain is the cortex, which resembles the brain of a reptile, one of the earliest life forms to evolve on our planet. This reptilian brain is concerned with the basic functions of life: survival, self-protection, and procreation. The cortex alerts you when your well-being is threatened and stimulates your fight-or-flight response. It is the seat of your identity as a separate entity and it governs the ego.

Superimposed over your cortex is another brain called the neo-cortex, or "new brain." The neo-cortex is so different from the cortex in form and function that scientists are still trying to figure out how it got here. All we know is that at some point in evolution about three million years ago, a radical shift generated a new and different kind of brain that grew around and over the old one. The neo-cortex is responsible for our higher intelligence, reasoning faculty, and ability to live cooperatively, with a sense of joy, purpose, and achievement far beyond survival.

When you observe an event and click into a survival response, you are operating from your reptilian brain. (I know this doesn't sound very romantic, but hey . . .) The cortex is your best friend when deciding which side of the road to drive on, how close to stand to the edge of a cliff, and keeping an eye on your kids in a crowd. But if you apply a fight-or-flight mentality when your survival is not truly threatened, you generate unnecessary upset and lose sight of how to handle the situation appropriately. Behold one *big* reason your life sucks: You put up your dukes in situations that call not for war, but wisdom. You let fear call the shots at the expense of love. During the time since the neo-cortex has developed, life on the planet for humans has become less and less about survival and more and more about personal, social, intellectual, and spiritual expansion. Yet many of us think and act as if we are going to keel over if the car we want doesn't come in fuchsia or the hottie we just met doesn't return our phone call within the hour.

We find a significant clue to our life purpose by examining the size ratio of the neo-cortex to the cortex: 105:1. The new brain is *105 times* the size of its primal predecessor. This means that we are designed to use over 99 percent of our brain for interesting pursuits such as figuring out how to hook up your surround sound home theatre, pick one of the 93 credit card offers you got in the mail today, and reading *Far Side* cartoons; and less than 1 percent for keeping your arms inside the roller coaster car. So if you are spending more than 1 percent of your thought wondering how you will pay your rent or if you will still be breathing after the New Jersey Turnpike, you are taxing your poor cortex and underusing that hefty new gray matter designed for getting the best deal at Nordstrom's.

In spite of our brilliant ergonomic design, our culture still emphasizes struggle and down-plays ease. Our boss proudly justifies his position by reminding us how long he sweated to get where he is. Yet his 20 years of struggle may not have been required by life, but by his belief. If he believed it took 10 years to become a manager, that's how long it would have taken. When good things happen fluently and easily, we tend to apologize as if we have not paid the requisite suffering. Meanwhile, others become wealthy or successful in a short time, they love the adventure, and serve many people in the process. Richard Bach wrote *Jonathan Livingston Seagull* in a few weeks. Bill Gates became a billionaire in a few short years. Julia Roberts rose to the top of Hollywood's A-list in her early 20s. Tiger Woods turned the golf world upside down before he was 21. Are these people just lucky? Did they violate the "no pain, no gain" edict? No, they just trusted their inspiration and did what they loved to do the most. Then, empowered by passion, they attracted the people and resources to assist them.

Refusing to play the struggle game does not mean that you sit around on your duff and wait for someone to hand you a fat check. It means that when you feel a sense of struggle welling up within you, you stop, step back, and ask yourself, "Is there an easier way I could do this?" Am I pushing against something more than I need to? Is the universe giving me a message to approach this from another angle? Usually you will find that the wall you are hitting is directing you to find a door down the way a little. Sure, you can take a sledge hammer and pound the wall down brick by brick; but why waste your time and energy when there is an easier way to get the same result?

Success requires attention, investment, action, trust, honesty, self-confidence, persistence, determination, focus, teamwork, resolving differences, learning from mistakes, and commitment. Note that this list does not include struggle. Struggle is something we superimpose over a natural flow. Remove struggle from the equation, and you will see clearly what to do. It is all much easier than you have been making it.

You Thrive on Drama and May Be Addicted to It

When I was a child, every day at 12:30 my mother would religiously turn on the TV to watch *Queen for a Day*. On each show three women competed to see who could tell the biggest sob story. Every day I heard about fires, desertions, divorces, deaths of spouses, bankruptcies, hospitalizations, kids in trouble and a smorgasbord of other calamities. Every contestant would break down into tears, while the mustached host stood by with a bottomless box of Kleenex. At the end of the program the audience would vote by applause for which woman's story was the most pathetic, and she would win a washing machine.

The only thing more pathetic than the contestants' stories was the show itself. If Emmy Awards were given for "Most Dysfunctional," *Queen for a Day* would win hands down. The program glamorized victimhood and rewarded contestants for drama. All for a stupid washing machine. The show is long gone, but the game goes on like a bad soap opera that outlives all its actors.

Have you ever noticed that people who have a lot of drama in their lives, always have a lot of drama? And people who have little drama in their lives, always have little drama?

And people who have a moderate amount of drama in their lives, always have a moderate amount?

Drama is a choice. It is not forced upon us by fate; it is an experience we generate. If you have a lot of drama in your life, there are several likely reasons: 1) You grew up in the midst of drama, with parents or siblings whose lives were turbulent; you learned to expect drama and keep finding it; 2) You are addicted to adrenaline; if you suddenly found yourself feeling peaceful for more than a few moments, you would feel bored, fidgety, or disoriented; 3) You are receiving some kind of reward or "points" for your drama, such as attention; an excuse for not achieving your goals; the satisfaction of being "right" in a conflict; gain of money or material support for misfortunes; an escape from distasteful work or relationship; or finding acceptance and security in a peer group of others whose lives are also dramatic and who identify themselves as victims.

Certainly challenging and upsetting events befall all of us; it would be naïve to expect anyone to go through life without disappointment or distress. The question is: How much mileage do you get out of a disturbing event when it occurs? How many times do you tell the same story? How apt are you to turn a momentary upset into a life-threatening issue?

A woman named Stephanie came to me for counseling during a rocky time in her marriage. She was quite distraught and felt that she could not go on in her tumultuous relationship. Our counseling soothed her, and she got back on track with her husband. Later she went through a stormy divorce that centered around a harrowing tug-of-war over child custody. During this time I received numerous phone calls from Stephanie, who was always at the end of her rope. I did my best to calm and support her. Then her husband stole the children. Then she got them back. Then the couple got together again. Then they broke up. Then she stole the children from him. Restraining orders were flying in all directions, and someone was always violating them. Then she met a man who took her away from it all, but stole her money.

At first I was very worried about Stephanie; I would get balled up trying to figure out how to defuse her crises. Later I realized that she thrived on the drama of her life. Stephanie had many choice points where she could have chosen a less dramatic route, or at least interpretation, but she enjoyed the thrill of living in a perpetual cliffhanger. Eventually I recognized that the best way to help Stephanie was not to try to end her dramas, but to just accept, appreciate, and support her for who she was and whatever she chose. Stephanie was going to do what she was going to do, and she would learn what she was going to learn. I think I was more worried about her than she was worried about herself. Eventually I realized I could not afford to be attached to her choices or their outcome.

You can blow trivial experiences into epics or reduce huge challenges to simple data. I met a woman named Jenny who recounted to me how her twin children had once been kidnapped. While the experience was quite harrowing when it occurred, Jenny had come to resolution with it and extracted from it many important lessons, including a deeper appreciation for her children. I was astounded by the calmness and clarity with which Jenny told her story; her account was brief and she exuded a positive attitude about how much she had gained from the event. By contrast, I have heard more distress, fear, and disorientation from some women who have broken a fingernail. Is drama a fact of life, or does it exist in the mind of the beholder? Emerson noted, "No man ever stated his troubles as lightly as he might."

We have been so conditioned to believe that life is based on drama, that the notion of a drama-free life is radical, even heretical. You might even feel insulted by the suggestion that you have a role in the dramas you experience. But it is so. You are powerful enough to create any life you choose. If you enjoy your dramas, then admit it and carry on in high style. If your dramas are making your life suck, then it's time to look at alternatives.

Begin by considering that your life can be passionate, colorful, juicy, adventurous, sexual, sensual, intimate, romantic, stimulating, rewarding, and immensely successful without drama as a required element. Then, when something dramatic begins to happen, ask yourself, "Do I really have to give up my peace for this? Is this truly a survival crisis, or can I handle this in a matter-of-fact way? Do I really need to take this personally? Is there a positive lesson or gift in this experience?" Your response to a potential drama can intensify it or defuse it. The perspective you choose makes all the difference.

Just because you shine in a crisis, doesn't mean you need a crisis to shine. You may have built your self-image or self-esteem on being a firefighter, but you don't have to go out looking for fires to have an identity. There are all kinds of ways to feel alive besides emergency, and there are many routes to self-worth beyond that of savior. If you are going to save anything, make it your sanity. Then you will be in the best possible position to help, while turning your melodrama into a mellow drama.

You Settle for Less Than
What You Want or Need

I took a day trip with my friend Joseph and his sister Geri along the magnificent Big Sur coastline, a breathtaking journey winding along many curves overlooking a passionate sea sculpting a wave-worn coast. Every now and then we would ask Geri what she wanted to do. To my surprise, she never stated her opinion. "Would you like to get something to eat?" we asked her. "If you are going to stop, I will," she answered. "Would you like to have a look at this beach?" we asked. "Whatever you like," was her response. Finally Geri became nauseous from riding along the curvy road. She was lying down in the back seat of the car, her face a pasty green. "Would you like us to pull over so you can rest?" we asked. "No, that's all right," she answered. "You can just keep going." (And she wasn't even Jewish!)

As our day went on, I realized that Geri had lost her voice of self-expression. She did not know how to ask for what she wanted. Geri had been married for 40 years to a man who made all the decisions for the family. He was not a domineering man; the couple had simply established their relationship on an unspoken agreement that he chose and she went along. Over the course of 40 years of saying, "Yes, dear," Geri had lost touch with her own choices to the point that when she was asked what she wanted, she was unable to verbalize it.

In my seminars I have encountered many women in the same position. They get married at a young age, live for their husband and children, and eventually become strangers to their own hearts' desires. Then, at the age of 40, 50, or 60, their husband leaves or dies, and they are utterly lost. Some do not even know how to write a check. Running their own lives is as alien to them as piloting a space capsule.

A similar phenomenon occurs among men who lose their wives at an elderly age. Men who become dependent on their wives, often die soon after their wife dies. Statistics show that women live longer after a husband dies, than men do after a wife dies.

The hidden gift behind the sudden departure of a spouse is that the shock serves as a wake-up call. I have seen many women, after their initial disorientation, become motivated to take charge of their lives. They reclaim pride in their physical appearance; lose weight; don stylish clothes; start their own business; enroll in stimulating classes; and travel. I have likewise watched men get in touch with their feelings; participate in communication seminars; go out dancing; develop rewarding hobbies; and remarry. The end of a marriage does not need to be the end of a life—it can be the beginning!

The most powerful way to break the long-time habit of swallowing your opinion is to practice speaking your truth impeccably. When you are asked what you want, do not utter the pat answer that wants to automatically roll off your tongue. Instead, pause for a moment and tune into your honest response. Find the place in you that feels good about a particular choice, and verbalize it. You might ruffle a few feathers or ultimately not get your choice, but in most cases you will end up far ahead of where you would have been if you did not speak up. *Asking for want you want increases your chances of getting it.* And even if you don't, you will enjoy the satisfaction of living true to yourself. You will avoid shrinking a little bit every day until your life is the size of a thimble.

In my seminars, participants often ask, "How can I find my life purpose and live it?" I tell them, "Start telling the truth with a passion, especially about the 'little' decisions of daily life. How can you expect to know and live your life purpose if you don't even tell the truth about which restaurant you want to go to for dinner?"

Are you social, or honest? Are you a people-pleaser, or a soul-pleaser? Are you moving ahead toward your dreams, or are you busy trying to fit your unique jigsaw-puzzle piece into a space that doesn't match it? As you live more and more authentically, you attract other authentic people, and the jigsaw space you find will complement theirs. Your honest words and actions will broadcast a signal that magnetizes the right partners and events.

A sales and marketing convention for an internationally successful corporation took the theme, *"Think Big—Settle for More."* This motto does not say, "Struggle for more," "Manipulate for more," or "Battle for more." *Settle for More* means that you set the bar at your desired standard and you do not shrink back in the face of fear, habit, or history. You craft a large cup in your mind and invite the universe to help you fill it. You keep remembering the ideals that make you feel best, and you use them as your guide. As W. Somerset Maugham noted, *"It's a funny thing about life; if you refuse to accept anything but the very best, you will get it."*

Sometimes when life is not delivering your immediate goal, it is helping you to not settle for less than your greater goal. Several years ago I needed to move my office. I wrote down a half dozen required attributes for my ideal facility and enlisted a real estate agent to search on my behalf. He showed me a space that I liked, but the rooms were small and the building was located at a noisy intersection. Since I was under the gun to move and the place was otherwise adequate, I told him I would take it. He told me he would get me a contract in a few days, and I assumed the deal was a shoe-in.

When the contract did not arrive after a few weeks, I began to get edgy. I needed to move in a short time, and if this deal did not come through, I would not have time to find another place. I called the realtor and asked him what was happening. He sheepishly told me that the landlord did not like the kind of work I do and he did not want to rent to me. I grew angry and gave the realtor a piece of my mind. "That's discrimination!" I snarled, and hung up. Now what would I do?

Later that day as I was driving home, I felt an urge to take the scenic route via a picturesque country road. I followed the inkling and soon came upon a dear old country store with a "For Rent" sign in the window. I inquired with the owner, a lovely lady who was thrilled at the idea of having my business in her building. The space was larger than the office that had fallen through, the rent was less, and it was in a lush and tranquil tropical setting just a few minutes from my house. Bingo! In retrospect, I was glad that I did not try to force the issue on the first rental. It was not what I really wanted anyway. I had started to settle, but my deeper intention was so strong that the universe responded to my real desire. Life was assisting me even when it appeared it was working against me.

You Get Stuck in the Past

When you resurrect the painful past by recounting it, you drag a stinky dead animal onto today's banquet table and taint the sparkling now moment. The only place the past exists is in your mind; it has no reality or control in the present unless you fuel it with your attention. Your past cannot haunt you, but you can haunt yourself with it. Give yourself a break and let it go.

If you are trying to undo a past behavior pattern, there are two ways you unintentionally keep it alive: The first way is by *judging and resisting* it. What you resist persists. If you keep bringing it up, it will keep bringing you down. Guilt is resistance to the presence of love, persecution turned inward. (A good definition of guilt is, "punishing yourself before God doesn't.") If you want to make sure you keep doing something, just keep feeling guilty about it. If you want to remove its hold on you, find evidence for your innocence. Keep trying different perspectives on for size until you find relief. Try to understand why you were drawn to the behavior. Perhaps anyone who had the experiences that led up to that behavior might have chosen the same route. Was there any good that came out of the experience? Did (or do) you actually enjoy it, but according to societal standards, you are not supposed to? Have you learned through the experience? Are you stronger, wiser, deeper, or more compassionate? Did the experience and its results move you to a new place in your life that you would not have come to otherwise? How would someone who truly loved you view the behavior? Do *anything you can* to shift your regard of the event(s) from judgment to compassion and empowerment.

The second way you keep your past in force is by broadcasting it. The more you call others' attention to it, the more you reinforce its power over you. Now their thoughts, feelings, and expectations are added to the mix. I am not suggesting you hide your past; just don't dwell on it and misuse the power of the word against yourself. And don't spend most of your time on a first date telling your date why your past relationships have failed! If you do, you just set your new relationship up to fail. I went out with someone who told me, "Every man I have ever been with has left me." Well, so did I. Program your new relationships to go where you want to go, not where you've been. You really don't need to explain all your dysfunctions to your new partner—let him discover them himself. And if you let yourself be new, he may not discover them at all. He may discover someone entirely more wonderful than you believe you are, based on your past tainted with self-judgment. Instead, talk about where you are now and the path you would choose. Build a positive, exciting vision of you and your relationship and invite your partner to step into it with you. You cannot change your past, but you can change how you think about and deal with it, and that makes all the difference.

You also undermine your potential by letting your expectations be programmed by the negative experiences of others. Why let their past determine your future? If you have friends who have had gnarly divorces; a sister on a vendetta against your parents; a colleague who has no kind words for the I.R.S.; or anyone who is angry and upset about anything, you may be influenced by their negative viewpoint and go on to attract the same experience yourself—not because that's the way it is, but because that's what you expect. I once worked with a fellow with whom I had an excellent rapport. Later I discovered that many people in his industry did not like him; they called him a flake and a cheat. One of his former clients called me and told me not to work with him. But my personal experience with him was quite positive, so I refused to allow their experiences to color my interaction with him. We went on to have a great business relationship.

A more subtle way you allow the experiences of others to program your life is by treating statistics as facts rather than opinions. Anyone who cites a statistic has an investment in the statistic; it is quite rare to hear a statistic from an unbiased voice. If you have ever taken a class in public speaking, debate, marketing, or statistics, you know how easily statistics can be manipulated to persuade listeners to a speaker's point of view. In *It Ain't Necessarily So: How Media Make and Unmake the Scientific Picture of Reality,* authors Murray, Schwartz, and

Lichter explain that most of the statistics you read as breaking news stories are provided by companies who want to sell you something. When you read, "An independent laboratory has found . . .," the laboratory is rarely independent; it was most likely commissioned by a company with an investment in a particular result. Before believing or acting on a statistic, find out who reported it and what they might be getting out of it. Statistics generate opinions, but more often opinions generate statistics. We do not believe what we prove; we prove what we believe.

The most heinous use of statistics I have seen showed up on a large sign at a metropolitan airport. The sign, sponsored by a cancer organization, blared, "By this time in five years, ___ out of ___ of you will not be in the picture." (I have replaced the numbers with blanks so as not to perpetuate the inference.) The sign showed photos of 20 faces, with a certain number blacked out to indicate they would be dead of cancer. I felt repulsed by this ad. The sign was programming a belief that would burrow into the subconscious of the hundreds of thousands of people who would view it, and contribute to the continuity of the statistic—in a way, a self-fulfilling prophecy.

You may justifiably argue that a statistic is simply a statement of the way it is; a certain percentage of people do die of cancer, and this is a fact. But facts are always evolving. They are not solid entities at all; they have a life span, disintegrate, and give way to new facts, sometimes quickly. Sir James Jeans noted, "Science should give up on making pronouncements. The river of truth has often turned back on itself."

Consider these facts, circulating on the Internet, that were realities 100 years ago:

- The average life expectancy in the U.S. was 47.

- Only 14 percent of the homes in the U.S. had a bathtub.

- Only 8 percent of the homes had a telephone.
  A three-minute call from Denver to New York

cost $11. (Multiplied by the factor of inflation, that would be about $219 today.)

- There were only 8,000 cars in the U.S., and only 144 miles of paved roads. The maximum speed limit in most cities was 10 miles per hour.

- The average wage in the U.S. was 22 cents an hour. The average U.S. worker made between $200 and $400 per year. (That's an average of $6,000 by today's standards.)

- More than 95 percent of all births in the U.S. took place at home.

- Most women only washed their hair once a month, and used borax or egg yolks for shampoo.

- The population of Las Vegas, Nevada was 30. The remote desert community was inhabited by only a handful of ranchers and their families.

- Plutonium, insulin, and antibiotics hadn't been discovered yet. Scotch tape, crossword puzzles, canned beer, and iced tea hadn't been invented.

- There was no Mother's Day or Father's Day.

- One in ten U.S. adults could read or write. Only 6 percent of all Americans had graduated from high school.

- 18 percent of households in the U.S. had at least one full-time servant or domestic.

- Marijuana, heroin, and morphine were all available over the counter at corner drugstores. According to one pharmacist, "Heroin clears the complexion, gives buoyancy to the mind, regulates the stomach and the bowels, and is, in fact, a perfect guardian of health."

- Some medical authorities warned that professional seamstresses were apt to become sexually aroused by the steady rhythm, hour after hour, of the sewing machine's foot pedals. They recommended slipping bromide—which was thought to diminish sexual desire—into the woman's drinking water.

These statistics sound ridiculous now, but they were quite real in their day. One day the statistics we live by now will seem equally fantastic. One day the percentage of people who die of cancer will be negligible and we will look back on our current death rate with as much curiosity as we consider the Las Vegas population of 30. Someone will find a cure for cancer; or people will not expose themselves to carcinogens; or people will recognize the link between stress and disease, or . . . who knows? But the day will come. One morning you will wake up and read in the newspaper that cancer is no longer a threat. That day could be any day, perhaps even tomorrow. That is why posting a statistic like the one in the airport is a huge dis-service, for it purports that today's reality will apply in five years. Likewise, a doctor who cites a statistic prognosticating how long you will live in the face of a particular disease, is being honest but not truthful. Honest because that is the fact as it applies to most people; untruthful because it may not apply to you.

Statistics and actuarial tables work because most people live predictable lives. They are influenced by the same news-casts; read the same billboards; consume the same fast food; attend the same schools; listen to the same sermons; take the same drugs; agree with people of the same skin color; oppose the same political party; fight over money; complain about the same problems; and are willing to settle for a cookie-cutter life. If you fall into this category, you can rely on statistics to predict your future. Yet there is another option:

*You can live from choice
rather than default.*

You can heed your inner spirit instead of the herd. You can form your opinions on what you feel and know rather than what you hear. You can change your destiny from a statistic to an ecstatic. A statistic is a photograph of what has been. If you want to be a has-been, believe in statistics. If you would rather dwell in possibility, do not invest your attention in the realities others have created. Invest your attention in what you would create. Only then can you truly call your life your own.

If you approach life with the belief that it sucks, it stands little chance to be wonderful. If you approach it with the expectation that your good can and will come to you, it will be extraordinary. Henry Ford noted, "Think you can or think you can't, and either way you'll be correct." Albert Einstein put it this way: "There are only two ways to live your life: one is as though nothing is a miracle, and the other is as though everything is a miracle." Miracles come to the miracle-minded and dramas befall the drama-minded. Miracles and tragedies are both interpretations, and interpretations craft experience. Your life will shrink or expand according to your expectation. Whatever size cup you bring will be filled, so make it a big one.

YOU GET FOOLED BY Appearances

My friend Lina was a television star on a popular Canadian soap opera. She was cast as a selfish, manipulative prima donna—the kind of character you love to hate. When Lina left the television studio after broadcasting each day, fans of the series would be waiting on the street and curse her out for being such a bitch. In real life she is a lovely woman, nothing like her television character. But the fans were sucked into her performance. They believed she was her role. They lost their peace over a person who did not exist.

Lina's viewers' predicament is not so different from the way we get tripped up in real life. We see an appearance, judge it, react to it, and then live as if it were so—even if it robs our happiness. Then we get others to agree with us and rail against it, throwing more logs of fear and anger onto the pyre. We can waste hours, days, and even years of our life running from or fighting against something that does not truly threaten us—or even exist! If you keep getting sucked in, your life will suck.

To triumph over the seduction of appearances, we must, as the film *American Beauty* hinted, "look deeper." While I was conducting a weekend seminar, we began our Saturday morning program with a warm-up circle dance. As I gave the directions, one young lady in the group couldn't seem to get the hang of the dance; she was confused and kept missing the steps, which threw off the people near her. I began to feel impatient and told her several times to pay attention. I guessed that she did not really want to be at the program and her mind was wandering elsewhere. Later she mentioned that in order for her to attend the seminar, she had to work the night shift at her supermarket job. She had participated in our Friday evening program, worked all night, and came directly to the seminar Saturday morning. My judgment about her was entirely wrong; it wasn't that she didn't want to be there; she wanted to be there so *much* that she sacrificed to make it so. I lost my peace and criticized her over an invalid interpretation. Every time you lose your peace, you have made an invalid interpretation.

In the Bible we are told, "Judge not by appearances." Appearances fool us into thinking that we and the people in our life are defective or evil, and others seek to use or hurt us at the first opportunity. Certainly there are people who might do this, but the vast majority are trustworthy and supportive. Most people are honest, want to be helpful, and prefer to get along. If you are tempted to argue that people are evil and life is about surviving, you are making a case for keeping yourself in such a world. You probably live with a sense of fear and mistrust, compounded by armoring your heart, which hurts you more than anyone else and causes you to miss the love you seek.

Consider an alternative perspective: Everyone carries within them a spark of the divine, which comes forth as we acknowledge it. Our sense of being defective, needy, and powerless is a mass hypnosis to which we have acquiesced.

We have been programmed to see life as a sea of troubles, while it is an ocean of possibilities. Well-being is far more prevalent than pain. You are not sinful, but innocent. The people in your life want the same things as you do and bring you not threat, but gifts and opportunities to awaken, grow, and love. There is ample supply of everything you could want. Your life is not a problem to be solved, but an adventure to be enjoyed. You are doing better than you think.

If the above vision of life sounds preposterous or naïve, you have succumbed to the nightmare that keeps the illusion of lack and separation in force. To wake up, get your life back, and reclaim your right to happiness, read on.

How You Get Fooled by Appearances and What You Can Do

You Think Looking Good Is More Important Than Feeling Good

By the time Audrey was 18 years old she had not grown breasts. Feeling self-conscious and inferior, she decided to get breast implants. Soon after her surgery, Audrey realized something was wrong and she returned to her surgeon for correction. Over the next 32 years, Audrey underwent seven more surgeries to alleviate problems with her implants. Finally, at the age of 50, Audrey died on the operating table in the process of correcting her breasts.

Fortunately, Audrey flat-lined for just a few minutes and then she was resuscitated. When she regained consciousness she realized what had happened and she decided to have her implants removed once and for all. A month later Audrey faced a large group at one of my seminars and, with tears streaming down her cheeks, reported, "I stand before you today for the first time in 32 years without falsies or implants. I am flat-chested, but very much alive and happier than I ever have been. I have finally realized that my life is worth more than my breasts." Audrey instantly received a standing ovation from the entire audience. (The next day she received an extraordinary love poem from a man in the group.)

To what lengths will you go to look good at the expense of feeling good? When you put appearance before substance, your efforts usually backfire. When I was 15 years old I took a summer job in a factory. I hardly ever got outside and rarely made it to the beach. By mid-summer I looked rather pale. So I went out and bought a tube of instant tanner. I rubbed the ointment on my arms and face and looked forward to impressing my coworkers. On Monday morning I strutted into the shipping department, feeling very cool. The first greeting I heard was, "Hey Alan, what's that orange shit on your face?" So much for instant tanning.

Looking good is important. I respect people who make an attractive appearance and I try to look as nice as I can. Certainly you will go a lot farther in the world if you create a positive presentation. The problem comes when looking good becomes so important that you stop feeling good. A strong question to ask yourself when striving to look good is, "Am I doing this by my own choice, with a sense of joy, or am I motivated by fear or pressure? Am I proceeding from an internal 'would,' or an external 'should?' Who is running my life, anyway? Can I look myself in the mirror and like not just what I see, but *who* I see?"

Another aspect of looking good is trying to look cool. Instead of buying breasts, you might buy a prestigious home; drive a flashy car; land a corporate power position; seek to be seen with influential people; or amass numerous degrees. All of these endeavors, as well as cosmetic surgery, are fine if they bring you inner joy and you would do them for yourself even if no one else ever saw you. But if your motivation is to impress others, you will ultimately depress yourself. One day you will arrive at the crossroad between authenticity and image management. You will have to decide whether you are here to please the world or your spirit; other's demands or your delights; proving yourself or being yourself.

When you keep spirit first, you look great as well. To find truth in a world of illusion, reverse what unhappy people tell you about how to get happy.

Looking good doesn't always lead to feeling good.
Feeling good always leads to looking good.

Certainly you might contend that looking good helps you feel better about yourself. That's cool. Do it. But the real test of self-love is to feel good no matter how you look. Then you really soar! A woman who attended one of my Hawaii seminars felt very self-conscious about being overweight. For years Jessica postponed her joy until the day when she would lose 30 pounds. But somehow that day did not come, and she was miserable. Then one day she decided to find beauty in her body as it was. Jessica asked a photographer in our group if she would take some nude photos of her, just for her. The two women went out into nature and did a photo shoot. Jessica returned glowing. She was one of the happiest people I have ever seen. Instead of trying to fit her body into someone else's idea of beauty, she decided to call it beautiful now.

Another woman at a retreat was embarrassed about having had a double mastectomy. Early one morning she invited another woman and a man to accompany her to a beach, where she ceremoniously disrobed and revealed her body before them and God. This ritual was her way of accepting her body and coming out from hiding. Her guests were honored to be a part of her revelation, and they supported her wholeheartedly. She returned to the group as if she had been reborn.

I am not pushing nudity. I am pushing unconditional self-acceptance. Since many of us, especially women, have experienced painful issues around body appearance, your most valuable transformational tool is to love your body no matter what condition it is in. When you can stand in front of the mirror naked and appreciate who and what you see, you are well on your way home.

There is something about someone who is in love with him- or herself that makes you fall in love with them, too. My friend Elsita, at age 96, is one of the most vibrant, vivacious women I have ever met. She is quite healthy; her skin is hardly wrinkled; she frequents parties with people half her age; she is deeply in love; she recently published a book of her original poetry; and she gives impassioned public readings. Elsita explodes every myth about what is supposed to happen when you get old; she is not old on the outside because she is not old on the inside. Elsita leads with her heart, and her health, beauty, and well-being follow naturally.

Unhappy people set criteria for love which are always just beyond their reach. Happy people make loving now more important than reaching for anything out there.

The only thing you can't afford
to postpone is joy.

You Believe There Is Not Enough

Every problem you experience stems from a thought of lack. Lack of money. Lack of love. Lack of time. Lack of available men or women. Lack of passionate sex. Lack of health. Lack of affordable housing. Lack of well-paying jobs. Lack of respect or support from others. Lack of safety. Lack of trustworthy people. We perceive lack and then make choices from a position of "not enough." But the tricky thing about any perception is that it is self-fulfilling. You tend to see more and more of whatever you focus on. You can cast the spotlight of your attention on scarcity long and strong enough that you end up living in a wanting world—not because it is so, but because you have engineered it.

Several years ago on the island of Maui a *tsunami* (tidal wave) warning was issued. Immediately many local residents ran to the supermarkets and bought all the rice off the shelves. Fortunately, the tidal wave never occurred, but there was a shortage of rice on the island for weeks. The problem was not that people bought rice; the problem was that people bought more rice than they needed. In fear of shortage, they hoarded it. The irony is that the hoarding *created* a shortage. If everyone would have bought just what they needed, there would have been enough for everyone. The universe did not create the condition of lack; it was created by people acting out of fear.

Hoarding rice is similar to hoarding weight. Being overweight is not always a physical issue; it is emotional. Body fat is a reserve in case of future famine. But it is not physical famine we protect against; it is feeling emotionally unsupported. If you are carrying more weight than you want or need, ask yourself, "What was happening in my life during the period I put on weight?" Usually there was some emotional trauma such as child sexual abuse; the divorce of parents; the death of a parent; a radical or frequent change of residence; your own divorce; or a business setback. Suddenly you felt alone and vulnerable, and you tried to bolster your sense of security by holding weight.

The answer to overweight is not so much dieting as it is moving from a sense of insecurity to inner security. There are thousands of diets that work, yet most people regain the weight they lost. This is because overeating is a symptom, not a cause. Heal the issue at the emotional level, and the physical aspect will follow naturally. (When I vacationed in Bali, I lost 10 pounds in two weeks. I wasn't even trying to lose weight. I went to banquets and ate rich desserts. Why did I lose weight? I was having such a good time that when I lightened up emotionally I lightened up physically.) Recognize that you are safe and your happiness does not depend on people or events. It is quite natural for a child to equate their security with their parents, or a young wife to look to her husband and marriage as a source of well-being. Yet your source of security runs far deeper than your parents or husband. Your true foundation of security lives within you. You can fulfill your dreams with or without supportive parents or a spouse. You are capable of nurturing yourself and drawing nurturing people around you. No matter what has happened in the past, you are now in a position to make self-honoring choices.

Discover the crucial relationship
between your beliefs and your experience,
and you will dump the programming
that has made your life suck.

When you are upset you are affirming lack, and when you feel good you are recognizing abundance. As you recognize that life is rich and you are rich in it, scarcity-motivated behaviors have no purpose and fall away spontaneously. When I placed a bird feeder outside my house, the first bird to discover it was a beautiful red cardinal. The little fellow sat there, happily chomping away at the seeds until another bird showed up. Quickly the cardinal pecked the other bird away, claiming the feeder as his territory. Several other birds arrived, and the larger bird fought them all off. I sat with some friends, watching and laughing. There was much more seed in the feeder than that one bird could eat in a month! Yet he was protecting the supply as if there were not enough. Even if the seed ran out, I had more to replace it. In essence, the bird had access to an unending supply, but acted as if it was scarce; he wasted time and energy fighting to guard something he could not really lose.

People who try to convince you of lack always have an ulterior motive. Have you ever noticed that nearly everyone in the media who tells you that you have a problem, has something to sell you to offset it? One of the oldest marketing techniques is to convince people of what is wrong with them and then offer them something to fix it. Those who stand to gain from your "problem" will try to underscore how bad off you are. The more frightened and needy you feel, the more you are motivated to seek safety and relief. It is rare that someone in sales gets excited about how well you are doing and wants to celebrate it with you without presenting you with something to buy.

During the gasoline shortage in the 1970's I went to a local Honda dealer and looked at the new fuel-efficient Civic. After I inspected the car, the salesman told me in an ominous voice, "You'd better make an offer today. Tonight President Carter is going on television to announce gas rationing. Tomorrow morning there will be a long line of people vying for this car, and who knows what the price will be then."

A chill of panic rippled through me. Maybe I should snag the car now before the ravenous hordes swoop down, I wondered. But something inside me spoke, *"Relax. Don't worry. Don't let yourself be intimidated by fear."* That voice felt more real and comforting than shrieking desperation. I told the salesman I wanted to shop around some more and I would take my chances.

That night President Carter announced gas rationing. I continued to shop. A week later I decided on the Honda and returned to the dealership. There I found the same car I had looked at, still on the showroom floor at the same price. The next day I drove my new car home, my satisfaction doubly sweet for acting from faith rather than fear. (Later it was revealed that there was no gas shortage at all; oil producers fabricated it to jack up prices.)

Never act out of scarcity or panic. Do not allow yourself to be pressured into doing something you do not want to do or are not ready to do. Never let anyone frighten you into a decision. If you do, you will surely regret your action. Then you will have to retrace your steps and undo what you did from a position of "not enough." Instead, proceed from choice. Act when you are ready to act. Wait until you have come to a decision that works for you. If it's not a "Hell, yes!" it's a "Hell, no!" Associate with friends and business colleagues who are motivated by a positive vision rather than panic, hustling, or emotional manipulation. As you trust your inner knowing, your decisions will honor you and your intentions.

There is another group with an investment in your troubles: people immersed in victim consciousness. Why? Misery loves company. By convincing you that you have a problem, they get to keep theirs and all the sick rewards that accompany a "poor me" mentality. They are looking for pity partners. If you do not agree that you are deficient, they may accuse you of living in denial. But it is they who are in denial of their strength and power to create the life they would choose. If someone becomes upset with you because you will not agree with their notion of what is wrong with you (or them), you can be certain they are a prisoner of a scarcity mentality. Your greatest gift to them and yourself is to stand firm in the knowledge of your wholeness.

You can reverse lack thinking in your business and put the abundance principle to work for you. See yourself as an agent to help people get what they want. There is a world of difference between answering a need someone already has, and creating a need so you can fill it. My friend John Stemet is a very successful real estate agent. Unlike many realtors, John has an easy-going attitude and enjoys his work and life immensely. He told me, "I don't sell real estate; I help people make their dreams come true." I have done several real estate transactions with John and watched him place service and integrity above manipulation. Once, as I was about to close a purchase, John did some detailed research and found a defect in the property that rendered it unsellable, which killed the deal and John's commission. But it endeared him to me forever. He may have lost one sale, but he gained a lifelong customer, as well as those I have recommended to him. We can all apply this model to our career. Dub yourself a Dream Manifestation Agent, and watch your career take off.

Recognizing a prosperous universe takes the pressure off your transactions and makes them an adventure. For every need you have, there is someone out there who can fulfill it. For every service you offer, there is someone who can use it. If you are seeking a job, there is someone who can use your skills and pay you for them. If you want to sell a car or home, someone is looking for one like yours; life is always seeking balance, and your need and theirs are a complementary match. As you relax and trust that the universe has ways to link people who can help each other, the transaction will unfold in the right way and time. Patience and faith always pay off. *Do not act out of desperation.* You are not desperate, you never have been, and never will be. Desperation implies that life cannot supply your need. But it can and will. Things always work out, especially when you don't try to force them.

You Get Involved in the Dark Side of the News

During a recent five-year period, homicide arrests in America decreased 13 percent. During the same period, coverage of homicide on the three major television networks increased by 336 percent. While public safety has actually improved, the media has created the appearance of it getting worse. News reporting is highly selective in favor of tragedy. "If it bleeds, it leads."

If your life sucks, quit giving your power away to data that a narrowly-focused industry is filtering to manipulate your emotions for the sake of selling detergent. A radio talk show host described the news as "a proctologic view of life." Most of the news that is reported as the events of the day represents a tiny portion of what actually happened that day, generally the worst and the waste. The garbage in your trash can is not a fair representation of your life, and the daily news is not a fair representation of life on the planet. Abraham-Hicks suggests that the media be allowed to report what happened on a given day only in proportion to everything that happened that day. So if you live in a city of one million people and there was one murder in the city that day, that event should be allotted one-millionth of the newspaper or telecast. Instead, a murder gets five minutes out of a 30-minute broadcast, which creates a very disproportionate sense of what occurred in that city that day. Very rarely does the news take into account all the people who had a fulfilling day; enjoyed their children; made love; took a walk at sunset; netted a new business contract; or had friends over for dinner, enjoyed a glass of wine, and laughed together. That is not newsworthy.

If you need to know about something, you will. Major stories have a way of finding you, and if the information is important to you, you will have easy access. I'm not suggesting you bury your head in the sand; just don't bury it in mass fear. Ultimately, mass media is not responsible for the preponderance of disaster consciousness; end users are. If people didn't get so involved in public drama, the news would have to find something else to deliver. For an experiment, a large city newspaper published two different editions of a day's news. One headline broadcast a local murder trial, while the other heralded a breakthrough in peace talks in the Middle East. The murder headline outsold the peace talk headline by a factor of four to one. As long as readers and viewers are titillated by aberrant behavior, we will get more of it.

There is a way to make the news work in your favor: selectively sift through the news and use it for inspiration, not desperation. Find articles that help your business or give you stimulating ideas for self-improvement. If you read about a loss, think about some way to turn it into a gain. I learned about a philanthropist named Milton Petrie who read the news each day to find out who needed help. One day he read about a beautiful young model whose boyfriend had knifed and disfigured her face. Mr. Petrie called the woman to his office and presented her with a check for $1,000,000 so she could have restorative plastic surgery. The next day he made a large donation to the family of a policeman who was recovering from being shot. Can you imagine the joy this man felt to help these people? You do not have to be a financial millionaire to turn the news around. You have a full palette of thoughts, words, prayers, and acts at your disposal, all of which are very powerful and more effective than money. The news of the World Trade Center attack, horrible as it was, generated an outpouring of love, caring, and generosity unlike any this country or the world has ever experienced. Millions of concerned people donated vast amounts of money, service, blood, skills, prayers, and support for those directly affected by the disaster. Behold a marvelous example of taking dark news and transforming it into a venue to open our hearts and to share our resources, which are infinite.

Quit talking about disasters at the water cooler. Don't read the newspaper or watch the news while you are eating. What you think and feel while you eat profoundly impacts your digestion and health. If you wake up to a clock radio, set it for a time other than the hour or half-hour, so you awake to music rather than who got squashed overnight. Don't watch the news just before you go to sleep. (And you wonder why you aren't sleeping well?) The thoughts and feelings in which you immerse yourself before you retire set the stage for your dreams, how well you rest, and how refreshed you feel when you awaken. The last thought you think before you go to sleep is the one that ruminates in your subconscious throughout the night and emerges as the first thought you think when you wake up—so make it a good one.

To sleep well and awaken refreshed, use your evening, or at least your last hour before sleep, for relaxing. Listen to beautiful music; read your favorite book; talk about something enjoyable with your partner; cuddle with your kids; step outside and gaze at the moon and stars; take a short walk; pet your dog or cat; or do a spiritual practice such as meditation, yoga, or tai chi. One very simple yet extremely effective practice is to list your appreciations for your day. Think of all the things you are grateful for and then note them in a journal or share them with your partner. This will open your mind and heart to a good night's sleep. (If you have trouble sleeping, read one of Amy Dean's books, such as *Pleasant Dreams*.)

If you are going to do something with the news, create some good news. Contribute to the stream of thought that moves humanity to an ocean of infinite possibilities rather than keeping it spinning in a whirlpool. There is no such thing as a neutral or idle thought; every thought you think leads you to freedom or bondage. You may not have control over what happens in the world around you, but you have total control of what you make of it.

You Try to Fix Symptoms
Rather Than Address the Cause

It always seems easier to try to manipulate the symptoms of a problem instead of getting to its root. Much of Western medicine is focused on quick-fix pain relief rather than eliminating what caused the pain in the first place. Certainly if you are in pain, you want relief, and our medical system is very good at alleviating it when it arises. But wouldn't it be more valuable to get rid of it for good by removing its source?

Chronic pain, physically, emotionally, or financially, is a signal to look deeper. It is a wake-up call. If the same thing keeps happening to you over and over again, with different people in different places, the only thing in common is you. That's not fun to hear, because it is more attractive to blame your problems on the outside world than to accept responsibility for your role in your experience. But *if you spot it, you got it*. I had a problem with reading glasses. Every time I would buy some at Costco, after a month they would break at the hinge of the earpiece. For a while I complained about the shoddy craftsmanship. Then one day I noticed I had an unconscious habit of twirling the glasses while I was thinking. But the glasses weren't built for twirling. The problem was not with the glasses; it was how I was handling them. Likewise, I met a woman who broke her right ankle 11 times in various "unrelated accidents." Another woman in one of my workshops had been engaged three times, and each time her fiancé died before they got married. (I didn't ask her for a date.)

Diseases don't just happen to us; we participate in them. Something inside us sets up illness and sustains it. This does not make you wrong or guilty; it makes you powerful. If you are powerful enough to make yourself sick with your thoughts and attitudes, you are powerful enough to make and keep yourself well. One of the pioneers in claiming responsibility for total self-healing is Louise L. Hay. Many years ago Louise was diagnosed with cancer, which motivated her to delve deeply into her self-esteem issues. Louise went on to experience a profound and permanent healing through affirmation, prayer, visualization, and upgrade of thought, word, and attitude. Louise's bestseller *You Can Heal Your Life* identifies mental and emotional causations for many diseases, with positive suggestions and affirmations to reverse them.

I was visiting a friend who had been struggling for a long time with eczema. We looked up "eczema" in *You Can Heal Your Life* and found it was related to antagonism. I asked my friend if she was feeling antagonistic toward anyone, and she told me she was not aware of such an attitude. An hour later I casually asked her what was happening in her love life. She rolled her eyes, made a sour face, and blurted out, "I am about ready to slit my throat." She was feeling antagonistic toward herself! It's much easier to buy a skin cream than confront your feelings of antagonism. If the skin cream works and the rash goes away for good, you win right there. But if the condition persists, you are being called to look deeper.

The same principle applies in your world of finance. If your relationship with money is out of alignment, you run into money problems wherever you go. If so, the answer is not more money—it is more consciousness. You can get more money, but if you don't get more consciousness, the new money you get will go where the old money went. Instead of changing the shelves in your store or finding a new financier, change your mind. Upgrade your attitude. Tell the truth about where your passion lives. Quit complaining about what isn't working and build a solid vision about how things could work. Get on your own team. Invest your soul, and you will reap mega-returns.

To get rich, you have to think rich.
To think rich, you have to know you are rich.

There are many forms of riches beside money. You might be a millionaire without even knowing it! If you have health, loving relationships, laughter, appreciation for the beauty of nature, a relationship with your higher power, visionary ideas, time, talent, wisdom, caring, or kindness, you are very wealthy indeed. When you acknowledge that you are rich now, prosperity naturally follows. If you deny or overlook the gifts at hand, you crimp the hose through which prosperity is trying to flow to you. Striving to make more money without an attitudinal shift is like fighting for peace. You can't get there from here.

Facing and healing the source of a problem buys you far more relief than topical cures. If you assume 100 percent responsibility for everything you experience, you will have 100 percent power to create the life you choose. Then you will be the source of your own health, romance, and economy.

You Think You Are Just a Body

This is a big one for many of us. Our culture is so body oriented that we tend to lose touch with our spirit, which runs far deeper. Your body is important, but there is so much more to you! People who build their worth and identity around their body set themselves up for a great deal of pain. They are rewarded for how they look, not who they are—to the point that they believe that how they look *is* who they are. Then they attract people who treat them like a body only, and get sucked into a world of illusion. Then they wonder why their life sucks.

Of course you want to enjoy your body. Stay in shape; don your most fashionable clothes; wear makeup that highlights your beauty; get your navel pierced; eat the tastiest foods on the menu; romp in bed with your attractive partner; and place yourself in beautiful environments. Just remember, as you go, to keep your soul alive. Make decisions from your heart, not just your form. Try to see other people for who they are, not just how they look. You will always have judgments about things you like and dislike about your body and others'; we have been meticulously trained to do so. Yet you are greater than your judgments, and you can make choices from a value system higher than appearance. Some people look great but are spiritually vacant. Others look less glamorous, but glow with wisdom and joy. As author Antoine de Saint-Exupery eloquently noted in *The Little Prince,* "It is only with the heart that one can see rightly. What is essential is invisible to the eye."

One side effect of identifying with your body is the belief that you are fragile. You are not. You are strong, safe, and secure. Only your thoughts make you vulnerable to "the slings and arrows of outrageous fortune." When you regard yourself as breakable, you give control of your life to people and things outside you. But nothing out there can really hurt you. Even germs and bacteria cannot assert themselves into your experience unless you are open to them. Louis Pasteur, who revolutionized science and medicine by discovering bacteria, confessed on his deathbed: "I fear that I have made a big mistake. Now I realize it is not bacteria that cause disease, but the medium with which the bacteria come into contact." Bacteria can harm you only if you are an available host. You may not have control over what germs blow your way, but you have total control over your energy field, which either allows them into your system or keeps them at bay. The strength of your immune system is in direct relationship to your thoughts, attitudes, and alignment with your spirit. You could theoretically walk through a field of lepers and be untouched (and many have). I and many others have walked barefoot over 1100-degree burning coals and not been burned. Fear makes you weak and faith keeps you strong. And what is faith but the underlying knowledge of who you truly are? Have faith in your inner being, and no alien poop or goop can bother you.

The illusion we trip over most is death. Because we have been taught that we are bodies only, we assume that when the body dies, that's it. But the end of the frame is not the end of the game. Nature demonstrates with compassionate authority that death is but a stage of transformation. A leaf falls off a tree, decomposes back to earth, and becomes a new tree. A drop of water falls to a meadow as rain, nourishes a flower, and evaporates back into the sky where it re-forms into new droplets to feed new flowers. Talk about sophisticated recycling! Nothing is ever lost in the universe; it just keeps showing up in different and more interesting packages.

When anyone dies, no matter who they were or what they did, they go back to Spirit. Get over the eternal heaven or hell thing right now; it is all a fairy tale designed by people who want to control you by scaring you into doing what they want. Or to lead a life as boring as theirs, so they are not jealous of the fun you might have because you are not afraid. Heaven and hell are experiences you generate with your thoughts and attitude, right here, right now. In any given moment you can shift from hell to heaven (or back). Behold your power to shape your destiny!

You are more like a river than a rock; more of a flow than an entity; more electricity than wire. When you lay your body aside, your energy goes on, just like that of your loved ones who have gone on before you. They are not very far from you at all, and you will not be very far from those you love. If you think you are just a body, you will have a hard time recognizing your immortal nature and you will experience great anxiety. But if you are more of a force than a thing (Buckminster

Fuller exclaimed, "I seem to be a verb"), death is not a bad thing at all, and certainly not a cause for fear or sorrow. Death is not an end; it is a magnificent release. When someone we love dies, we grieve not for them, but for ourselves. They are in a good place; we are stuck in the appearance of loss. But just as the leaf does not lose as it becomes a tree or the drop of water does not lose as it becomes a cloud, we do not lose when we flow back into the great ocean of Spirit. Trust me on this: Nobody really dies. We just change addresses.

You Do Not Recognize Pervasive Well-Being

One evening on a lark my friend Dee and I went to shoot pool at a local billiards hall frequented by colorful local characters. Around 9 P.M. the lights in the building began to flicker and a minute later they went out. We looked out onto the street and saw no lights on anywhere. We were in the midst of a citywide power outage.

I started to feel uneasy as we stood in the dark in a tough section of town amidst a bunch of tattooed, leather-clad, body-pierced, Camel-smoking dudes who probably didn't read self-help books or meditate. I was just waiting for the crowd to bolt to go loot Wal-Mart across the street. (Yes, the thought of a new CD player did cross my mind.) I took a breath and decided to just trust. Then I watched all of these guys line up and pay for their time on the pool tables, patiently working with the attendant as he calculated their bills with a pencil and paper and took their money by flashlight. They could have easily just walked out. Despite my judgment based on appearances, these fellows were honest and integrous.

But the best lesson was yet to come. As Dee and I drove off and made our way through the city streets, we found that all of the intersection signal lights were dead, too. Thousands of cars coming from all directions would have to negotiate in the dark without crashing into each other. Again I felt anxious. How would we get home safely?

We arrived at the largest and most complex intersection in the city, with several lanes in each direction, plus left turn lanes. I watched with awe as all the drivers approached the intersection cautiously, came to a full stop, and took stock of all the surrounding cars, as if the intersection was a 4-way stop. Then each car carefully eased forward, courteously offering oncoming cars the right of way if there was any doubt who was to go first. We did the same, and found ourselves on the other side of the intersection with no hassle at all.

Each crossroad became an adventure in focus and cooperation. After passing through several crossroads, my apprehension gave way to delight and appreciation. People really knew how to work this out! Drivers were safe and respectful. In spite of potential chaos and confusion, every-one was maneuvering wisely and getting where they needed to go. I felt inspired and exhilarated!

Then we came to an intersection where a police car was parked and an officer was directing traffic. He looked quite frazzled in his attempts to get all the cars safely through the intersection. He was blowing his whistle, pointing, and waving frantically. And the cars moved through in an orderly fashion. But cars were moving through all the intersections in the city in an orderly fashion. Out of the hundreds of crossroads, there were only a handful at which police were directing traffic. Yet everyone was doing fine on their own. The appearance, based on the behavior of the officer I observed, was that if the police weren't there, pandemonium would ensue. But the police weren't there in most places, and pandemonium did not ensue. Mutual support, consideration, and teamwork ensued. People knew how to take care of themselves and each other. Even without signal lights, traffic was flowing very nicely.

I am not suggesting we do away with traffic lights or police; they do help. I am suggesting that traffic lights and police do not keep people safe. People choosing well-being keep people safe. We attribute undue power and responsibility to societal agents that seem to hold our world together, when it is really the intelligence and good will of people and life that keep the world functioning. The appearance is that police maintain law and order; the reality is that most people choose law and order. Laws and police do not stop people who do not want to be ruled by them; criminals are doing what they want to do anyway (a former car thief told me that "locks are for honest people"). Yellow lines in the middle of the road do not keep cars in opposing traffic lanes from crashing into each other; we would rather not crash, and the lines help us play out our choice. Doctors and medicine do not keep us healthy; we are each as healthy as we choose to be, and doctors and medicine assist us to maintain the level of health we desire. Government does not keep our economy humming; people just like to make money and spend it. Well-being abounds not because a few people are in charge of it, but because life is programmed for success, and those who flow with it enjoy its benefits.

Most things go well for most people, and the stuff that goes wrong is insignificant in proportion to all the things that go right. Millions of things have functioned productively for you today, but you have been trained to notice the few things that don't and build your experience around them. Any problem you recognize represents but a tiny blip on the radar screen of your well-being. Even while you are experiencing a difficulty, homeostasis is working on your behalf to return you to perfect balance. Your role is simply to relax and allow nature to take its healing course. Consider the miracle of healing a cut on your arm or leg, a process we take for granted. You do not have to actively heal yourself; if you just keep the cut clean and do not irritate it, within a few days your arm or leg will be restored to its original wholeness. And so it is with all of our problems; just get out of your own way and let universal intelligence work its wonders. Voltaire noted, "The art of medicine consists of amusing the patient while nature effects the cure."

On a macrocosmic level, the earth circles the sun at an extremely precise tilt and orbit; if it were off by a fraction of a degree, the planet would hurtle off into space. But the earth has maintained its course for billions of years, and will continue to do so for billions more. On a microcosmic level, consider the amazing Bush Turkey. The male Bush Turkey builds a large nest of leaves in which the female lays her eggs and then departs. The male then covers the eggs with more leaves and maintains the mound at the precise temperature of 92.4 degrees Fahrenheit. If the temperature drops below 92.4, he adds more leaves; if it rises above 92.4, he removes some. He has a perfectly-tuned internal thermostat to foster the birth of his children. He does not run down to Long's Drugs and buy a thermometer. He knows exactly what to do because universal intelligence operates through his natural instincts. When the young hatch, they find their way to the surface and without any parental interaction fly away within one hour. Mother, father, and children know their roles and play them out with seamless perfection.

Do you not think that you are at least as intelligent as a Bush Turkey? Can you conceive that universal wisdom is operating even when you are not aware of it? In spite of your doubts, fears, and resistance, life is conspiring to keep you happy, healthy, and successful. Your job is not to make things happen, but to let the movie roll—it's a two-thumbs-up flick with an ending you will love. The more you acknowledge that well-being abounds, the more well-being you enjoy. When media mogul Ted Turner donated a billion dollars to the United Nations, he affirmed, "The world is awash with money." Likewise, the world is awash with well-being. Life is designed to work. You can and will make it through any dark intersection. Everybody wants to get through it with you, and everyone will. Remember the truth and stand for it in the face of appearances to the contrary, and you may rightly call yourself a master of your own destiny.

YOU WASTE YOUR ENERGY ON THINGS THAT *Suck*

One afternoon an official-looking fellow showed up at my door and flashed an I.D. from the water department. "I just read your water meter," he told me, "and I have to inform you that you have an unusually high usage this month."

"High usage?"

"Yes, sir—about four times the usual amount."

"Four times?"

"That's right. Here are the numbers."

I looked at the numbers. He wasn't kidding.

"It's our policy to let you know about this in case you have any leaks in your water system."

Hmmm. No leaks I knew of. Maybe my tenant has been taking a lot of showers, I wondered. But 80,000 gallons of showers? Nope, he doesn't even wash his dishes. I thanked the waterman and told him I'd try to conserve this month and hope the bill would come down next month.

A few days later I was sitting on my back porch when I noticed a puddle in the corner of the yard. That puddle had been there for a while, but I figured it was due to some heavy rain we'd had. But the rest of the lawn had dried up. The puddle was still there.

I poked my hand into the puddle. There was a pipe beneath it, and it was leaking. I can tell you exactly how much it was leaking: 80,000 gallons a month.

If you are losing energy in the form of joy, health, money, or love, you have a leak in your system. There is no malevolent parasite that has invaded your world and is undermining you. Your leak is on your property, and you have access to repair it. The entire game of life is about making the best use of your energy. The question is not, "Is there life after death?" The question is, "Is there life *before* death?" To answer this for yourself—and live it—you must quit doing things that deplete your energy and start doing things that expand it. Moses delivered Ten Commandments that point to how to accomplish this, but A) Nobody wants to be commanded; B) Charlton Heston resigned as Moses to become head of the N.R.A.; and C) Nobody has enough patience on the Internet to wait for ten commandments to download. So here is everything you need to know to relocate from Suckville:

Do what brings you life.
Do not do what deadens you.

The reason you are not where you want to be is that you are doing things you do not want to do. If that sounds simple, it is. (One of the most popular tricks of power and control freaks is to hide in complexity. But the best answer to a problem is usually the simplest.) Sure, there are some things you have to do that you don't want to do, but not as many as you are doing. Give yourself a break.

*If you took the energy
you are wasting on things that suck
and used it for things you love,
what would you be doing differently?*

When you invest your time and energy in stuff that drags you down, you die a little bit every day. Then your life force reduces to a dribble and you croak. Yet the Bible documents people who lived for hundreds of years, and there are people in remote regions today who live far past 100. Their lives are simpler and they do not fritter away their life force watching people hit each other with chairs on Jerry Springer. They just live close to nature, eat yogurt, and develop meaningful relationships with llamas. So open your heart to a critter who won't dump you on national television and you will live long enough to get a birthday card from the President.

Everything you do is an investment in more of the same. The illusion is that if you do something you don't like long enough, it will go away. But the truth is that the more you get involved in something, the more involvement it leads to. (Ever own a boat?) If you truly enjoy something, dive in. If not, have the guts to walk away from what doesn't serve you. There is no redeeming value in misery (unless you do time-share presentations). The hell you worry about going to is not nearly as bad as the fear of it that drives you to do things alien to your spirit. If you live from fear, you already are in hell. If you live from love, you create the meeting point of heaven and earth.

How You Waste Your Energy on Things That Suck and What You Can Do

You Waste Your Energy on Activities That Suck

When you realize how precious your time is and how important it is to feel good about what you are doing, you will be very prudent about the activities you choose. I was raised as a people-pleaser; I believed that if someone asked me to do something, I was supposed to do it. But the more I lived to fill in the holes carved by others, the more I felt something was missing. That something, I discovered, was *me*.

In *Seven Habits of Highly Effective People,* Stephen Covey suggests, "Do what is important rather than what is urgent." How easy it is to get caught up in the emergency of the moment and lose sight of our dreams! You distract yourself because you realize that if you succeeded your life would change, and for many people the familiar—even if it sucks—seems safer than the unknown. The life you know may be painful and unrewarding, but at least it is dependable. You know who is going to hit you, how hard, when, and when it will be over. Prisoners of fear would rather stay holed up in the dungeon they have mapped rather than venture into an uncharted mansion.

Identity also plays a factor. If you have accepted a self-image as a mediocre player, you have to renounce it to step into a bigger persona. This can be difficult to do if your self-image is deeply ingrained. Once I set out on an airplane flight with a friend. My lecture sponsors had reserved a first class seat for me, while my friend had booked a coach seat. I arranged for her to sit next to me in first class, but when I invited her forward she sat with me for a few minutes, looked quite uncomfortable, and then returned to her coach seat. "This doesn't feel right," she told me in a timid voice before she left. "I just don't belong here."

The invitation to step into a grander life draws to the surface hidden insecurities and feelings of unworthiness. I have seen many people sabotage their dreams when they get close to having them. If you are unwilling to face your fears, you can find some ingenious detours. You will get caught up in all kinds of little things and set the important things aside for when you have the time. But if you don't *make* the time, you will never find it. In the end, everything you find is what you make.

You might be immersed in self-defeating pursuits because you would rather be right than happy. If you are attached to a victim position and you are reaping an emotional or material reward for your self-righteous indignation against people or powers that are keeping you oppressed, you might choose to stay downtrodden to prove your point. In so doing you clinch your lot as a loser. Your vendettas have a minimal effect on your oppressors, and a maximal effect on you. When you live in resistance, you undermine your creative potential and separate yourself from your mission and your joy. In the end, your mission *is* joy.

Take a piece of paper and write down the various activities you do in the course of a week or month. Then assign each a value according to whether this activity adds to your life or diminishes it. A value of +10 means it totally fulfills you and -10 indicates it totally depletes you. Then consider how much time you are spending in each type of activity. Right before you on paper you will see where and why your life sucks and where and why it is working. Then, next to each item, write down what step you could take to maximize what lifts you and minimize or eliminate what depletes you. Behold your road map out of hell.

You Waste Your Attention on
Things That Suck

While you may be very careful about what you pay for with your money, you are probably less careful about what you pay for with your attention. In the long run, how you spend your attention affects your life far more profoundly than how you spend your money. *Your attention is the strongest currency at your disposal.* If you squander it, your life will result in one big overdraft. If you invest it in things you value, you will collect interest big time—and be interested along the way.

A young warrior came to his tribe's medicine man and told him, "Inside my head two dogs are fighting all the time. One is wise and beautiful and the other is ugly and rabid. Which one will win?"

The medicine man answered, "The wise and beautiful one will win."

"How do you know that?" asked the warrior.

"Because that is the one you will feed," answered the elder.

Imagine two lawyers in a courtroom inside your head. One is arguing for your possibilities and you achieving your goals. The other is arguing for your limits and why you don't deserve what you want. Who will win? The lawyer whom you pay the most. The way you pay these lawyers, however, is not with money; it is with your attention.

Attention is energy. Whatever you feed it to, will grow. Attention is intention. Whatever you think and talk about paves the runway for what you will create. When you pay attention to things you want to happen, you increase the chances of them happening; the same dynamic applies for the things you do not want to happen. On a country road near my house, someone posted a huge sign painted in red letters on a large piece of plywood: *"Whoever Ran Over My Dog, Slow Down!"* The sign stayed up for over a year, until one day I noticed it had been changed: *"Whoever Ran Over My Son, Slow Down!"*

Every thought is a prayer, and worry is prayer in reverse. Calling attention to wrong-doings only increases their likelihood of happening again. Once you know what is wrong, mobilize all of your energy toward the solution. Problems are what you see when you take your eye off the goal. To pray effectively, keep your mind and vision on the end result you choose. Don't undermine yourself by being fascinated with the problem. Be fascinated with the solution.

The secret of genius is focus. If you can laser your attention on any subject or project, it will reveal its blueprint to you. George Washington Carver discovered 325 uses for the peanut and 100 for the sweet potato! Great geniuses are powerful focusers. Many have been called eccentric or insane because they put aside worldly concerns for the sake of their music, art, architecture, drama, inventing, or writing. But they are the individuals who change the world, while those with scattered attention wade through mediocre lives. Geniuses don't fritter their precious minds on mass trends. They create the trends that alter the masses.

Notice what happens when you point your attention in a direction. Read tabloid headlines while standing in line at the supermarket; recount your accident; or engage in gossip, and within a few moments you open the door to an entire realm of consciousness that matches your thoughts or conversation. Dwell on it a bit longer, and this becomes your reality, complete with agreement from others and facts that corroborate it. Then you feel depleted, you attract similar experiences that make you feel worse, and you wonder why your life sucks.

Then notice what happens when you focus on things you find rewarding. Read the words or biography of someone you admire; cruise into your art studio and grant rein to your creative impulse; spend an afternoon at the beach; or tell a loved one of your appreciation for them. Suddenly you find yourself feeling great and you draw unto yourself people and events that serve and empower you. All because you pointed your mind in a direction.

We live in a universe of infinite possible realities. At any moment any reality on which you place your attention will yield you entrée to it. Friend, go where you choose to go, not where you are dragged.

You Waste Your Words on Things That Suck

The Bible tells us, "In the beginning was the word." That's not just the beginning of the universe; it's the beginning of everything you do. If you recognized the creative power of the words that roll off your tongue, you would take care to concentrate on the things you want to come about. Your words create and your words destroy. When you verbally dwell on unwanted things, unwanted things dwell on you. When you focus on your desired visions, they find a home in your world.

Be sure your words match your intentions. Listen to what comes out of your mouth, and you will be appalled at how many statements you issue at odds with your dreams. You are probably making all kinds of statements that affirm why you can't have what you want. When your words (and feelings that accompany them) equal your intentions, your goals will manifest. The distance between you and your heart's desires is in direct proportion to how you speak about them. Come *from* your dream rather than heading toward it. The more conscious you become about your speech, the more you will direct your words in your favor. Eventually you will become a master creator and also recognize why the people around you are not getting what they want. Then you can help them by marshalling the power of your own word.

Complaining is a waste of energy, and utterly counterproductive. In a supermarket aisle I heard two women commiserating about their positions as housesitters. For a long time they traded stories about how inconsiderate their hosts were and how much they didn't like their jobs. I kept hoping for some positive words, such as some acknowledgement of something they appreciated about their work or their hosts; some constructive ideas about how they could improve their situations; or even a "This really sucks and I am going to find something I like better." But these two were utterly committed to misery; this was a black-tie pity party! I wanted to shake them and say, "Don't you realize how much you are hurting yourselves by agreeing how bad off you are?" But it was not my place to do so. They were steeped in their misery and found reward in glorifying it. They did not realize that in that moment they stood no chance of moving beyond it. My lesson from the experience, I surmised, is to be careful not to criticize without reaching for higher ground.

As soon as you become aware that something is not working, immediately shift your focus to the desired result. The moment you recognize "This can't be it," ask yourself "What *is* it?" and then mobilize all of your energy, including your words, in that direction. Problems are not bad at all; they are the beginnings of solutions. They exist for the very purpose of dislodging us from situations that fall short of our potential. Don't stop until you are ahead of where you started. Take your self-sabotaging speech and transform it into your ally.

You Waste Your Talents

People live unfulfilling lives because 1) They do not believe in themselves enough to express their talents; 2) They feel guilty about accepting money for their talents; and 3) They do not take action steps to build their livelihood around their talents. All of these situations are tragic. Such people end up doing things they don't really care about, they struggle materially, and wither emotionally because their life does not embrace their passion.

Our culture gives a great deal of credence to the caricature of "starving artist" and even romanticizes it. Two attitudes reinforce this debilitating image: The first is that our left-brain dominant culture does not value artistic expression as much as technical savvy. People who program computers get paid a lot more than those who paint the pictures that hang in their offices. Both are important. When money gets tight, arts programs are the first to be axed by the government, and arts proponents have to go begging to the private sector to survive. Yet there are cultures in which artistic expression is rewarded far more than intellectual prowess. The entire culture of Bali is devoted to the arts. Every person in the society is highly skilled at painting, woodcraft, stonecutting, fabric design, jewelry making, music, or dance. The Balinese live for art, and everything else they do seems to be an excuse to sustain them so they can go on with their artistic expression. As a result, the Balinese are among the happiest people on the planet. If we learned from their example and emulated it, we would be happier and our society would find more balance.

The second reason the starving artist myth stays alive is that artists buy into it. Young artists, writers, and actors believe they must live in a chilly basement, wear tattered thrift-shop clothing, purchase groceries with food stamps, drive a car made of more rust than metal, and hassle with their landlord every month over the late rent check. And so impoverishment rules, not because it has to be that way, but because *expectation is nine-tenths of manifestation.*

The key to overturning the starving artist syndrome is to observe and focus on artists who are not starving. Many artists have found a way to make a living through their craft, and they serve as redeeming role models for those with holes in their jeans. If you would like to get out of the basement and into a sunnier, more spacious place, study the lives of successful artists and get inspired by their achievements. You'll discover there was a time when they were in precisely your position. Then one day they were not. Hollywood A-List actress Renee

Zellweger had no idea how she was going to pay next month's rent when she received the telephone call informing her that she had been chosen to play Tom Cruise's love interest in the mega-hit *Jerry Maguire*. Harrison Ford showed up at his audition for *Star Wars* wearing his carpentry belt, on a break from his day job. Both of these actors rocketed to stardom overnight and never starved again. After rejections from 17 publishers, Richard Bach landed a contract with Macmillan, submitted his manuscript for *Jonathan Livingston Seagull*, and went traveling. When he came home he found a million dollars in his bank account. That's how quickly night can turn into day when you remain true to your inspiration and let the universe handle the details.

The other significant self-defeating behavior I observe in artists is their unwillingness to delegate or accept help with their business. Truth be told, most artists are not good business people. This is not a criticism, but a compliment to their artistic nature. On many occasions I have counseled artists, "Get someone to help you with your business!" There are lots of people out there who love to do spreadsheets, formulate marketing plans, and negotiate deals. They can do for you what you cannot do for yourself. If you hire one, they can do all the stuff that makes your head reel, free you to pursue your passion, and provide both of you with a good living. Quit whining, "I am just not good at business" or "I can't seem to get my work into a place where people will see it." There is someone out their whose jigsaw piece perfectly complements yours. Let them into your world and you will both thrive.

It's fine to wait tables or do telephone solicitation (just don't call me) while you are developing your artistic career. Just remember that you are doing this to support your dream and consider it a steppingstone to success. When I was in high school I took a menial job in a clothing store to earn money to buy my first car. I waxed the floor, scrubbed the toilet, and shoveled snow off the roof—all pretty gnarly tasks. But I remember the job fondly, for at the end of the year I drove away in my Catalina Convertible. I never lost sight that my labor was in the service of my deeper goal.

Something is bubbling inside you that would bring you rich reward to express. Your mission is to get in touch with it and do it. Until you do, you will sense that you are missing out on something big. And you are. If God made you an artist, then *be* an artist. Don't apologize or sell yourself out trying to be something else more lucrative or acceptable to your parents. In the end, the most lucrative career is the one that matches your heart, and the only acceptance you require is your own.

You Waste Your Energy on People Who Suck

Some people do things that suck. Or perhaps it's just the chemistry of your interaction that sucks. Some counselors would suggest it is important to hang in there in painful relationships until you transform them. Sometimes that's true. Sometimes it's not. Sometimes you need to just "make a new plan, Stan, and get yourself free." There must be 50 ways to leave your sucker. Here are a few of them:

People Who Really Suck

Some people are energy vampires. When you are in their company or after you depart, you feel drained, depleted, or depressed. They are emotionally or materially insatiable; no matter how much attention, time, or money you give them, there is always one more thing they need. If you try to help them feel better, they resist and argue for their problems. They don't recognize their ability to generate joy, love, or prosperity for themselves, so they look to others to sustain them. They may even appear cheery or say positive things, but below the surface their force field is like a psychic flypaper. Their mission statement is, "A first impression is a lasting depression." Comedienne Elayne Boosler advises, "Watch out for anyone who says, 'I have so much love to give and no one to give it to.' Immediately translate that into, 'I am the emotional black hole of the universe, and I will suck every ounce of life force from you if you let me.'" They walk around with a big invisible vacuum cleaner drawing protoplasm from all who enter their domain; show up and you will be consumed. You set out to be Jesus the savior, but end up as Jonah the dinner. Been there, done that, bought the t-shirt.

The best gift you can give an energy vampire—and yourself—is the recognition that they are whole, capable, and not in truth needy. You accomplish this not so much through words, but through attitude and action. Support them to stand on their own two feet and live from their strength rather than their perceived impotence. You don't help an alcoholic by buying them a drink, and you don't help an attention junkie by feeding their drama. They are asking for something deeper. They are calling for a higher vision than the one they are stuck in. While they are playing small, remember they are big. There are valuable lessons for them in whatever they are going through; the universe is inviting them to discover their inner power. Don't rob them of their lesson by getting caught in their arguments for lack. Keep your conversation brief and stay upbeat. If you must be in their presence for a period of time, make it your priority to feel good no matter what they say or do. Don't sacrifice your happiness for their upset.

No one really wants to be an energy vampire, and no one is by nature. Energy sucking is a learned behavior, reinforced by those who play into it. When needy people realize that their behavior is not truly getting them what they want, they will reach for more effective tools and find them. They are good people learning how to be self-generating. Their behavior is not a call for anger or resistance, but broader vision. Stay centered and alert with them, and "hold the high watch." Found yourself in your power and they will not be able to remove it.

People You Are with for the Wrong Reasons

When you engage with people who do not match your purpose or best interests, you will end up feeling sucked. Not by the people themselves, but by your own inner being telling you that you don't belong there. If you had followed your intuition, you wouldn't be there in the first place. Here is a list of people whose interactions will suck your energy because your presence with them is inappropriate:

- People you are with out of a sense of obligation.

- People who use, abuse, or don't appreciate you.

- People who don't want to be there.

- People you don't really like, but you want something from them.

- People with whom you do not set healthy boundaries.

- People you are trying to fix or save.

- People who don't like themselves.

- People whose friendships you have outgrown.

You can move beyond these toxic relationships by recognizing that 1) You have a choice about who you are with and why; 2) If this situation is not working for you, neither of you will end up with what you want; and 3) If you made an error by choosing to be with someone you don't match, you only compound it by continuing. Begin to speak and act on the truth that reverses the dysfunctional reason you got together, move on to a healthier situation, and you will both be better off.

People Who Don't Suck But You Think They Do

This is not attractive to consider—especially if you like being right about what's wrong—but it may be true and it might apply to more people than you realize. Your problem may not be out there, but in your perception. In this case your remedy is not to distance yourself from the other person, but to shift your attitude about them.

I had a friend who annoyed me every time I was with her. She talked constantly and always seemed to be in my face. But she was my girlfriend's friend and she spent a lot of time at my house. Once while I was fixing an upstairs window she stood at the bottom of the ladder and talked to me the whole time as if she was on a therapy couch paying me $200 an hour for my attention. But I was just trying to fix the window. I started to measure the window to see if she would fit through it.

Then one day while I was receiving a massage, this woman came to mind. Because I was in a relaxed and vulnerable state, I was able to see her through the eyes of appreciation rather than resistance. Suddenly I realized that she was not trying to hurt me; she just had a very strong personality. I realized that she really liked me and had always been very kind to me; I was the one who was trying to push her away. In that moment I dropped my resistance and I began to like her. From that time on, we enjoyed a very nice friendship and I did not feel that I had to run away from her.

You can transform any relationship by shifting your thoughts about it. This is where your true power lives. It is much easier to defuse limiting thoughts than to change someone or push them out of your life. Begin by simply considering something you like about the person or something kind they have done for you. Then try to not take what they are doing personally. Imagine that their words or actions are more of a statement about them than about you. If you can hold them a bit more lightly in your thoughts each day, you will be amazed at how your relationship will transform.

You Waste Your Energy on
Goals That Suck

Before you climb the ladder of success, be sure it is leaning against the right wall. Clever ingenious creatures that we are, we can attain anything we set our mind to. Before you set your mind to anything, however, make sure it is something you want.

Many people in our culture are clamoring—try panting—for fame and fortune. The gods of our society are not those with the greatest character, most penetrating intellect, or deepest peace of mind. They are those with the most money, best bodies, and sports records. (When was the last time you saw Dr. Stephen Hawking's face on a men's cologne ad or the Dalai Lama on the cover of *People*?) Our values are heavy on things and light on essence.

I know many people striving for success in the corporate world and the entertainment industry. Most of them are not happy campers. They are all trying to *get* somewhere, mostly at the expense of *being* somewhere. They live in a harsh world of judgment and competition and are constantly comparing their bodies, voices, or P & L statements to others. A friend of mine was being pursued by a certain man when she went to church each week. She was not interested in him and kept putting him off. Then one day when she left church he followed her out to her car, where he produced several of his recent tax returns with large numbers on them and tossed them onto the hood of her car for her to peruse. "Wanna go out with me now?" he asked smugly. "Even less than before," she told him as she got into her car and drove away.

Money, fame, a hard body, and first prizes are not healthy goals to pursue for their own sake. If you do, you doom yourself before you begin. You are building your house on sand, and when the first rain comes, you had better own a Speedo. Instead, allow these rewards to show up as by-products of following your spirit. Build your business or body because you enjoy doing it. Sing for your love of the song. Compete for the sake of honing your skills. What you do may look the same as the actions of those clamoring for approval, but the reason you do it and the way you feel as you proceed will be radically different. You will proceed from wholeness rather than inadequacy, and that will make all the difference.

Rather than designating a specific situation as your goal, designate a quality of experience. Don't pray or strive for a particular mate, job, or house. Instead, set your intention for the kind of relationship, job, or home you desire, and how you want to feel about it. Then leave the particulars to the universe. If you demand a particular form, you can get it, but you might miss the essence. I know a woman who intensely wanted a relationship, so she found a magazine photo of a handsome man and posted it on her refrigerator as a sort of treasure map. Within a short time she met a good-looking guy similar to the fellow in the photo and started a relationship with him. After a while it became apparent that he was an alcoholic, which ultimately ruined their relationship. Then she went back, looked at her treasure map photo, and realized he had a drink in his hand. She would have done better to focus on the *kind* of man she sought and the *quality* of the relationship that matched her heart's desires.

Specific goals such as a net income, ideal weight, or a slick car can be fun and useful; just *hold them lightly*. If you drive yourself crazy over getting them, when they arrive you will not enjoy them. Found your journey on trust, and the right things will show up and stay. When anxiety is your keynote, attaining your goal will not remove your fear, but only intensify it. *Struggle to get, struggle to keep.* Instead of striving for the Sale of the Century, enjoy the Sail of the Century.

In the end, the only goal worth seeking is a satisfied soul. This has nothing to do with what is going on outside you and everything to do with what is going on inside you. The more you try to find it out there, the less you find it in here. The quest for self-knowledge is especially challenging in a world obsessed with toys and external distractions. Yet if you commit yourself to discovering the jewel that glows within your heart, it shall be yours forever.

YOU KEEP
TRYING TO PROVE
Yourself

My tenth grade math teacher told our class a fable about a frog who sits on one end of a log and jumps toward the other end. The frog's first jump takes him halfway across the log. His next jump takes him half of the remaining distance. The frog keeps jumping, each time one-half of the remaining distance. "How many more jumps will it take," my teacher asked us, "before the frog reaches the other end of the log?"

We all took out our pencils and tried to figure out the answer, but no one could. That's because it was a trick question. The frog will never reach the other side of the log. He can get closer and closer and closer, but half the distance to his goal remains. Try as he might, he will never get there.

When you live or work to prove yourself to others, you become the frog on the log. You can feel like you are getting closer and closer, but you will never reach this goal. Your mission is doomed before you start because each time you leave something lacking. Even while you think you are winning, you are losing.

During a counseling session, I described my relationship with my father. When I finished, the counselor pointed out to me, "Your father was the kind of person who, if you did something 99 percent well, would point out the 1 percent you didn't do well."

His assessment hit me between the eyes; he was dead right. Suddenly I realized why I was never totally satisfied with anything I did. I had been living to prove myself to my father, which I could never do. You see, my father was never happy with himself. So how could I possibly please him?

Like many of us, I internalized my father's unattainable standards. The information I received during the counseling session was not so much about my father; it was about me. Since that time I have lightened up on myself. I have practiced giving myself credit for the 99 percent and giving myself a break for the 1 percent. Regardless of how my father lived his life, I still have the power to choose my own.

What would you be doing differently if you did not have to prove yourself to anyone?

I know a man who, at the age of 72, is still trying to please his 95-year-old mother. I have also worked in seminars with many people still trying to earn the approval of parents who are long dead. Authority figures, you see, live not in their bodies; they live in your brain. It is said, "It is impossible to defeat an enemy who has an outpost in your head." Your enemies are not your dysfunctional parents, childhood sexual abuser, or punitive parochial school teacher; your enemies are the thoughts they instilled in you that you still believe. It doesn't matter if your authority figures are living or dead, right or wrong, nasty or transformed; their influence exerts itself through your agreement with it—right beside your power to remove it.

Let's get one fact straight right now: You will never, never, never, ever, ever, ever, never, ever, never, ever, never,

ever, never, never, never, ever, ever, ever, never, ever, never, ever, never ever get everyone's approval all the time. Jesus didn't do it, nor did Gandhi or Princess Diana. Even very good people could not get everyone to like them. No one ever has and you won't be the first. You won't be able to get everyone to like any one thing you do, and you won't get any one person to like everything you do. So give up your quest for universal admiration right now; it is never-ending, infinitely frustrating, and it sucks. If you are ever going to receive the approval you seek, it is going to have to come from you.

How You Keep Trying to Prove Yourself and What You Can Do

You Are Living Someone Else's Dream

In the film *Out of Africa*, pioneer Karen Blixen confesses, "My biggest fear was that I would come to the end of my life and realize I had lived someone else's dream."

Is your life an expression of your heart's desire, or someone else's? I know a young man, Robert, who sweated through a year of medical school because his parents always wanted him to be a doctor. Robert's father took a second mortgage on their house to pay the tuition, and Robert felt too guilty to refuse. But he really wanted to be a teacher. This placed him in an awful predicament: While he was being trained to save other people's lives, he was losing his. By the end of his second semester, Robert fell quite ill, which motivated him to speak his truth to his father. His father was disappointed, but realized that his son would never be happy as a doctor, and he gave him his blessing to leave. Robert quit medical school and his health returned in a short time. He went on to become a teacher, which he loves.

Many people have all kinds of ideas about how you should be living, but they are do not matter unless they match your vision for yourself. Well-intentioned as others may be, no one knows your heart and destiny as well as you do.

The disease to please is a prevalent one. It shows up in the son who plays out his parents' hopes for the childhood they never had; the daughter who marries within the faith although she loves another; the wife who dares not defy her husband's wishes; the teenager anxiously striving to fit in with peers; the employee sweating to win the favor of his boss; religious adherents trying to be good so God will not send them to hell. But they are already in hell. If you deny your truth to fit into another's, you will find yourself there too.

If you want to get back in touch with your dreams and live them, these practices will help you:

1. Whenever you are about to respond to a request, ask yourself if your motivation comes from joy or duty. Is this your idea or someone else's? Would you be doing it even if someone else was not asking or urging you to? Is this a "should" or a "would?" Practice saying yes only if it matches your inner choice.

   Notice how activities that proceed from fear or obligation deaden you, while activities that proceed from joy or personal intention enliven you. Of course there are times that you choose to do something that would make another person happy, but there is a world of difference between you saying yes because you want to serve and support them and saying yes because you are afraid to say no. The important question to answer is, "Is this really my choice?"

2. Write a letter to each of the people you are still trying to please (even if they are no longer in your life). Tell them all of your feelings and everything you have experienced in your quest to please them.

Hold nothing back. Do not stop until you get all of your thoughts and feelings onto the paper. Finish with a declaration of how you would now like to be living instead. When you feel complete, burn the paper. It is not for them; it is for you.

You Measure Yourself Against an Impossible Standard

Some of the ideals you have been told you should attain are downright impossible. You might feel like the Greek mythological character Sisyphus, who spent eternity in Hades rolling a big rock up to the top of a hill, but as soon as he neared the top, the rock would roll back onto him. Talk about diminishing returns!

The only way out of Sisyphus's predicament is to give up the boulder rolling and celebrate your perfect imperfection. Let your process be as rewarding as your goal. If it's not fun now, it's not gonna be fun when you get there. And if you never get there, you will resent all the angst you suffered in trying. So whatever you are doing, enjoy it or quit it.

Men suffer under the *Gotta Get It Right* syndrome more than women. (That's why NASA began to send women up in space capsules—in case the crew got lost, *someone* had to be willing to ask for directions.) We men have been taught that we are supposed to know it all, and it's embarrassing to admit when we don't. Men also feel a lot of internal pressure to keep things working efficiently. This is why when a woman comes to a man when she is upset, the man thinks he has to solve the problem. But the woman doesn't regard her upset as a problem; she just needs to express her feelings. Finally the man throws his hands up in frustration and stomps out of the room, shouting, "I just don't understand you." If, in such a situation, the man can let go of his need to be a fixer and just allow the woman to vent, she will likely come out on the other side feeling better and he will save himself a bunch of stress. Women live longer than men because they don't carry the world on their shoulder and they express their feelings more freely. So men, let's take a clue, buy a few more years, and enjoy ourselves along the way.

Women have a different challenge: they have been taught they need to live up to an impossible societal standard for beauty. If you don't weigh 98 pounds, have a porcelain complexion, and your lips are not as puffy as a calzone, you aren't good enough. Meanwhile, the cover girls live on one lettuce leaf a day and go into cardiac arrest when they find a wrinkle. What a price to pay for glamour! Even the cover girls need help; *Playboy* magazine does a lot of airbrushing. Beauty is delightful to behold, but it's a vicious taskmaster.

Others are sweating to live up to religious standards with overbearing moral expectations. You would have to be a saint to live up to them, and probably a saint could not handle them either. (I think saints were a lot more human than we make them out to be; once they are dead we can idolize them and not have to deal with the human traits we would notice if they were present. One true mark of a good saint is their embracing of their humanity.) Morals are important, but if they wield tyranny, they suck. Robert Louis Stevenson suggested, "If your morals make you dreary, depend on it, they are wrong. I do not say give them up, for they may be all you have. But conceal them like a vice, lest they spoil the lives of better and simpler people."

The highest morality is personal integrity—living in harmony with your own value system. Religious ideals rarely encourage individual choice because they do not recognize that God guides people uniquely from within. Nor do they regard people as worthy enough to connect directly with God. So religions make up a long list of rules about how you should live, some of which apply to you and many of which don't. Religion helps lots of people, but others do better to develop a conversation with their own soul and forge a personal destiny. They find deeper meaning to discover their inner Bible rather than rely on one written by another. You cannot photocopy God; the more you do, the more blury the image becomes until it bears little resemblance to the original, and it becomes unreadable. Dogma insists that you adopt someone else's relationship with God, which is never as powerful as developing your own. We're back to the frog on the log. Sooner or later your karma will run over your dogma.

The only thing more important than being good is being real. More good comes from living your truth, than truth comes from living someone else's idea of your good. It has been said, *"It's not how good you are—it's how bad you want it."* Sincerity of intention attracts more success than seeking to satisfy externally imposed injunctions.

To get what you want,
be what you are.

Imitation sucks; authenticity rocks. Perfection is not a degree you attain; it is a truth you recognize. Find perfection where you are in who you are, and you will escape the ravages of the disease to please.

You Keep Trying to Fix Yourself

Fixing yourself is a task you will never complete because your quest is founded on a faulty premise. You cannot fix yourself because you are not broken. You can construct an entire world based on the belief there is something wrong with you and spend a lifetime trying to rectify it. If that scares you, it should. You might constantly question your motives, actions, and relationships, while the one thing you needed to question was the assumption that you are lacking.

The main thing wrong with you is the thought that there is something wrong with you. Your problem is that you think there is a problem. If you focus long enough on erroneous assumptions, they will confirm themselves. Then you will attract people who tell you what you have been telling yourself. Then your faults *really* seem real. But that does not make them real. It just proves that your mind is powerful enough to create a world and then live in it.

Your sense of inadequacy is learned. You were not born with it. You picked it up along the way, like chicken pox. Whoever told you there was something wrong with you suffered from the same delusion. Psychic self-abuse is a debilitating hereditary cycle that gets passed from generation to generation until someone decides to stop it now—that would be you. If you don't stop it in your life, your kids are next in line.

Little children have no concept of their defects. They run around naked; caress their genitals with glee; cry when they fall down; laugh ecstatically when they see something funny; ask for what they want when they want it; don't get embarrassed when they barf; play with anyone they like, regardless of age, skin color, weight, or adjusted gross income; and are fascinated if you pierce your navel or your clothes are from the '70s. Children live utterly unapologetically. They are motivated by delight, not approval. They don't need therapy because they don't question themselves. The goal of therapy is to reclaim the lost magic of childhood. We force children to trade their souls for public education, which renders them socially acceptable but spiritually impotent. The word "education" derives from the Latin *educare,* meaning, "to draw forth from within." In our culture, however, education often means, "to pound in from without." Musician Bob Marley proclaimed, "I have no education, just inspiration. If I were educated, I'd be a damn fool." You have been educated into your sense of not-enoughness. Are you willing to question it now?

If you look to psychology to help you fix yourself, consider that the Greek word "psyche," which is usually translated as "mind," actually means "soul." So psychology, in its purest sense, means "the understanding of the soul." But because we place our faith in the intellect more than the heart, much of psychology has been reduced to a study of the mind alone. You are so much more than your mind! Your spirit is immensely more real and powerful than the thoughts that ruminate in your brain, thoughts that have been largely programmed by people who want to sell you penis enlargements and push-up bras. If you try to heal the mind without honoring your soul, you set out through a long dark labyrinth that ends behind where it began. You will spend a lot of time and money mud wrestling with your adopted demons while you drag your loved ones on a wild ride to nowhere.

Real therapy goes far beyond fixing what is broken or trying to fill in a black hole that only keeps deepening. Therapy at its best is an adventure in peeling away the illusions that have kept you small, which leads to revealing your innate genius and beauty. If you are going to undertake therapy, look for these qualities in a therapist, which also apply to a good teacher, minister, counselor, mentor, or coach:

1. A good therapist draws forth the best in you rather than continually directing your attention to what is wrong with you. When you walk out of a session, do you feel lighter, freer, and stronger, or do you feel stuck and confused?

2. A good therapist is relatively happy and healthy. While it is unfair to expect a therapist to be a paragon of perfection, their demeanor should demonstrate the kind of attitude and energy you aspire to experience. "Never buy hair grower from a bald-headed salesman."

3. A good therapist is authentic and walks their talk. Their life reflects the values they express and suggest for you. They acknowledge that they, too, are on a journey of awakening. Sometimes you can learn more from a therapist's humanity than their

philosophy. A good therapist engenders a sense of shared learning and stimulates your sense that you are both on a similar path.

4. A good therapist strives to move you through the therapeutic process as quickly as possible and get you functioning under your own steam. Be wary of therapists who try to keep you in therapy for their own purposes. After seven years of primal screaming, a friend of mine informed her therapist that she felt healthy enough to move on. "Oh, no," the therapist answered. "We are just beginning to get into the real work." If you expect therapy to take a lifetime, it will—not because it must, but because you expect it to.

5. A good therapist sets appropriate boundaries. When they say no if you ask them to cross their boundary, they are teaching you to say no when you need to do the same.

6. A good therapist assists you to contact your own inner wisdom. You are the brilliant work in progress, not the therapist. They acknowledge that you know your own answers and their role is to help you develop the skills to unearth them. They will never try to force you to follow their direction. They may suggest and guide, but the choice is always yours.

7. A good therapist acknowledges that you are a multi-dimensional being. Their therapy program addresses all levels of your life rather than just one. They respect your mind, emotions, body, and spirit, and support you to nourish all these aspects of yourself and keep them in balance.

8. A good therapist places service and healing before money, power, or sex. They are there to serve, not to feed their ego.

Real therapy guides you past analysis to celebration; past survival, into creativity. Healing is just not about coping, but expansion. Many people find the richest therapy in petting their cat, salsa dancing, or playing basketball. Whatever leads you to feel good is therapy. Just do whatever it takes to feel truly happy, and you will be connected to all the wisdom you need to bring your visions to life.

You Compare Yourself to Others

Self-comparison is a direct route to hell. For every person you are better than, there is one better than you. The desire to be better than another springs from a sense of inadequacy. If you recognized your worth and wholeness, you would not need to regard someone else as inferior so you can feel superior.

To wake up from the self-comparison nightmare, recognize that everyone can be all they are without infringing on anyone else. Authentic self-expression does not take away from others; it empowers them.

There is room at the top
for everyone.

There is one very juicy and lucrative market that no one else can ever get their hands on. It is a market that you can corner right now and reap huge dividends for the rest of your life. The market is called *you*. No one else will ever be able to tap into that precious resource, and if you play your cards right, you can capitalize on it big time.

I received a strange comment from a fellow who referred to me in a motivational speech he delivered. He reported that he had attended one of my lectures, and I had violated 8 out of the 10 rules he had learned in public speaking class. But, he confessed, I was his favorite speaker because I was the most authentic. I took it as a compliment. When I speak, my goals are to 1) inspire myself; and 2) enjoy myself. If I succeed, the audience accompanies me on a great ride. If, on the other hand, a speaker is scared, bored, or doesn't love their subject matter, the audience doesn't stand a chance. You might as well bring out the cots before the speaker steps onstage. President Robert Taft noted, "The only statistic I can remember is that if all the people who go to sleep in church were laid end to end, they would be a lot more comfortable." I may not be a textbook public speaker, but I'm a wholehearted me. Somehow that works.

Rather than envying the victories of others, surf on them. Put yourself in their position and share their delight as if their triumph were your own. The word "envy" sounds like the acronym "N.V." ("New Vision"). When someone succeeds at something you desire, they are demonstrating that your goal is attainable, and because it has come into your awareness, you are that much closer to attaining it yourself. *There is no private good*; a win for them is a win for you. As you practice win-win thinking, your energy will shift and you will draw unto you the success you yearn for—not at the expense of others, but side by side with them.

You Sell Your Soul for Public Recognition

If you are enamored with riches and fame, you are setting out on a rickety bridge—not because riches and fame are bad, but because they are unworthy goals in and of themselves. Fame and glory are natural offshoots of expressing your passion and talents. If you pursue stardom for its own sake, your quest will crush you and you will miss the joy of the journey. *The road to glory sucks unless you choose a road that is glorious.* If you sell your body or soul to maneuver yourself into the public eye, you will have people sit in an audience to look at you, but you won't be able to look yourself in the eye. Build your own character, and you will attract people and situations worthy of your loftiest goals.

I know a singer whose lifelong ambition was to see her name in lights in Las Vegas. Her life was a constant struggle, filled with angst and drama. She was always about to sign a deal which fell through at the last minute. She was constantly fending off producers who wanted to sleep with her. Her voice was never good enough for her. She was not a happy person. Her desire for public attention twisted her soul in knots.

I also know of an 11-year-old girl who was playing around on her computer designing some clothes for her Barbie dolls. She showed her program to her father, who thought other kids might like to do the same. They took the program to the Mattel Toy Company, who liked it so much that they paid the child $1.1 million for the rights to the program. And she wasn't even trying for riches or glory. She was just having fun doing what she loved.

There are two types of people who become famous: those who pursue attention and those who pursue their passion. If you try to make it big without making it real, you are in for big trouble. If you make it real, you will make it big. Your name may not become a household word, but at least it will be a good name. If your name becomes a household word at the expense of your happiness, what a poor bargain you have struck.

If you need other people's adoration to feel like a success, what you are really seeking is your own adoration. Wouldn't it be sad if you got millions of people to love you, but you never learned to love yourself? Everyone called Elvis Presley "The King," and he died on the throne. Elvis had a good heart and he was a great entertainer, yet living up to a royal reputation is a heavy onus for any man to bear.

Even if no crowd ever flocks to see you, if you respect yourself, you are popular indeed. The happiest people are those who enjoy their own company. They don't need praise or followers; all they need is who they are. If you can find beauty and worth in your life as it is, you have found the pearl of great price.

If you want to become rich, make it a game. Do it for fun, not life-or-death. I know a very wealthy and well-respected man who owns several successful businesses. When I asked him what he does for a living, he laughed and answered, "I channel money." This fellow doesn't take money too seriously; he plays with it. He owns his goals; they don't own him.

If fame is your fortune, use it as a tool to deliver gifts. Some performers, such as Robin Williams, have kept their spirit alive in the midst of an industry that eats souls for breakfast. Robin chooses roles that deliver positive messages and he brings laughter wherever he goes. While filming *The Fisher King* in New York City, one scene was shot in Grand Central Station overnight. The shoot was on a tight schedule to complete by dawn, and this complex scene called for hundreds of dancers to perform a waltz in the train station. When technical snafus caused the actors and extras to sit around for long periods of time, they grew grumpy. At that point Robin, the star of the movie, wandered through the station cracking jokes, amusing the fatigued cast and crew. On another shoot, while filming *Patch Adams* on the campus of the University of North Carolina in Chapel Hill, Robin went into a local college bar one night and spent several hours spontaneously entertaining the students. Although he is a mega-star, he took the time to lift others along his way.

Riches and fame are highly seductive; they rarely turn out to be what they appear. Some of the richest and most famous people in the world are the unhappiest. And some are very happy. It's not whether you are rich and famous that makes or breaks you, but *how* you are rich and famous. If you are doing it to prove yourself, you will never win. If you seek to follow your heart without demanding a result, you are good to go.

You Collect People-Trophies

If you do not believe in your own worth, you may try to gain value vicariously by associating with people whom you feel are better than you or have what you want. People-trophy collecting falls into several categories:

- *Groupie.* You fixate on an idol and then immerse yourself in their world. You join their fan club, wear t-shirts with their photo, frame their toenail clippings, follow them around, fantasize about them, and give up your identity for theirs. Cute for teenagers, but doesn't become anyone over 18.

  A friend of mine is a massage therapist at a luxury resort. One day she phoned me and reported, "I had a brush with greatness today . . . I massaged Dustin Hoffman." Of course I wanted to hear about her encounter. Yet something struck me about her languaging: "My brush with greatness" sounded as if greatness was outside of her, and she was lucky enough to touch it for a moment. Framing the event in that way denied the greatness within her. Yes, Dustin Hoffman is a great actor, but she is a great massage therapist. Dustin Hoffman could have just as honestly called a friend and told him about his brush with greatness at the spa.

  If you are going to admire someone, retain your power as you do it. Respect role models who inspire you, but respect yourself at the same time. Instead of brushing with greatness, brush *from* greatness, and the magnitude you encounter will be your own.

- *Trophy dates or spouse.* You choose women or men who will draw attention and recognition to you. They are famous, powerful, rich, or beautiful. You are seen in public with them to impress others, and if your drive is strong enough, you marry your trophy. Prognosis: shallow, brief, and repetitive.

- *Starfucking.* This is the Hollywood term for sleeping with famous people. You may not be getting any acting jobs, but at least you screwed somebody who is. Self-esteem by import.

  Starfucking is not limited to Hollywood or the music industry, it occurs in every social clique in which some people are regarded as more important or powerful than others. Are you spending time (or money or sex) with this person because you like their company, or because being with them will lead to something else? You may be able to sleep your way to the top, but once you get there, the only way to go is down.

- *Name-dropping or Photo-dropping.* You collect direct or indirect associations with famous people. You're not sleeping with them, but when your friends walk into your house, the first thing they see is the photo of you shaking Alex Trebek's hand. Nearly every time I have been invited to a party in Los Angeles, the host mentions that Drew Barrymore or Keanu Reaves or someone of similar ilk "said they might come."

  Of course it is a treat to meet famous and talented people. But would you go to that party anyway? Would you go for fun and because you like the host? Do you need to get something from someone in order to make your attendance worthwhile? You don't need to rub elbows with fame to get somewhere. Just *be* somewhere. If you respect yourself enough and act from confidence rather than need, people will want to come to a party to meet you.

You don't need to sleep with someone, drop their name, or plaster their photo on your forehead to be important. You are important. Live from that importance, and important people will find you. And if you never met anyone famous, who cares? What you are looking for is not in Hollywood or at the top of the corporate food chain. It is in you.

You Are Fighting a Grudge Match

If someone hurt or defeated you and you are driven to succeed in order to get even with them, they are still defeating you. When you sacrifice inner peace for revenge, you have bestowed your enemy with total power over your life. The best way to get back at them is to renounce your bloody quest and live your life to the fullest.

During one of the recent Olympic games I watched a television documentary about a swimmer who in the previous Olympics had lost a gold medal by a fraction of a second. This fellow was so angry about his slim loss that he vowed to win in the next Olympics, and he devoted his entire life to training for the win. This documentary filmed and interviewed the swimmer at intervals during the four years between Olympics. As I watched the film clips, I was stunned by the fellow's intensity. I admired his discipline and tenacity, but in a way his quest was a sad one. While he founded his entire self-esteem on that win, he seemed obsessed, almost possessed. His life hinged on the next contest, and I don't think he enjoyed many moments in the interim. When he went on to win the gold medal, I breathed a sigh of relief—I didn't want to think about what he would have done if he lost again. Yes, motivation to win is important, and so is persistence and determination. But not at the expense of your happiness. If joy is the only true measure of success, this fellow's win was not whole; he traded four years of his life for that one moment—and set himself up for the next angst-ridden quest. In the film *Cool Runnings,* a coach told a similar contestant, "If you're not good enough without the medal, you won't be good enough with it."

I also saw a program about "The Human Barbie." A woman who was dissatisfied with her appearance had undergone 118 cosmetic surgeries, at a cost of over a million dollars, to get the looks she wanted. When asked why she had done this, she explained that she derived great satisfaction from "dissing men at parties" who, before her surgeries, had not paid attention to her. Self-esteem gained by revenge is no gain at all. It is self-loathing projected outward, then denied behind a curtain of "victory."

If you are motivated to succeed in the profession your parents warned you against; show up your elder brother in football; crush the company that fired you; or marry again quickly to prove that the jerk who left you made a big mistake, think again. When you set out on a vendetta to get back at anyone, they own your soul. *Fuggetaboutit!* If you are going to succeed, do it for you. Choose goals because you love them, not because others hate them. Do what you would do if no one else ever watched or cared. Do it because you care. As medical intuitive Carolyn Myss noted, "What you do is not as important as why you do it."

You will never win at proving yourself. Lots of frogs are trying to reach the end of the log, but very few own the log as they jump. Forget about proving yourself, and just *be* yourself. People who do not understand you will not settle for any proof, and people who appreciate you do not need any proof. Who and what you are is self-evident. As Emerson declared, "Who you are speaks so loudly that I can hardly hear what you are saying." Explaining, justifying, and defending are emotional quicksand; the more you try, the deeper you get sucked in.

Many years ago I went to visit a couple I wanted to impress. After dinner I renounced my dessert and went into the kitchen to do the dishes. Every now and then I whistled or made extra noise to let everyone at the dinner table know I was in the kitchen doing good. The final item I faced was a large oily wok. I will really do good now, I thought, so I took a big piece of steel wool and scrubbed the wok until it was shiny as a mirror. Just then the hostess came into the kitchen to see what had happened to me. Like a five-year-old boy showing his mom a finger-painting he drew in kindergarten, I held up the wok and exclaimed, "Look, Christine, I cleaned your wok!" Her eyes opened big as saucers and her jaw dropped almost to the floor. What I did not know, in my quest to do good, was that the wok was *supposed* to be oily. The oil seasons the wok and makes food prepared in it tastier. "It took me three years to season that wok!" she exclaimed. That was the last time I did good.

Now my intention is more to be real than good. It's a funny thing; lots of good comes from that. As I relax into my own rhythm, I am more attuned to the needs of others, and I end up serving far more powerfully than when I tried to do good according to some external standard. Discretion *is* the better part of valor, and authenticity is the better part of discretion.

YOU SAY YES WHEN YOU *Mean No*

In December 1945, a farmer near the Egyptian city of Nag Hammadi discovered over 50 scrolls of mystical Coptic writings dating back to 140 A.D. The passages were a collection of sayings of Jesus, some of which are included in the New Testament, and many of which are not. The writings have come to be known as *The Gospel of Thomas*.

One of the most compelling of these lessons (paraphrased here) teaches:

> *If you bring forth what is within you,*
> *it will save you.*
> *If you do not bring forth what is within you,*
> *it will kill you.*

I see many people dying a little bit every day because the life they are living on the outside does not match who they are on the inside. I have also seen many people regain their life force quickly when they tell the truth about who they really are and what they want to do. The game of life is to bring your outer expression into harmony with your inner truth.

I had a secretary who did not know how to say no. She would say yes to everything I asked her to do, and then just not do the things she did not want to do. This was a problem. One day I asked her if she would stop off on her way home and pick up a replacement ink cartridge for the office printer. She agreed, I gave her the store's address, and off she went. An hour later she phoned me to ask where the place was. By the time she arrived, the shop was closed.

The next day she tried again, and again I received a call from her. "I misplaced the address," she reported. I gave her the address again, and this time she arrived before closing. But she had forgotten the company credit card.

Finally I went into town and picked up the cartridge myself. My secretary wasn't stupid; in the office she performed complex computer tasks brilliantly. She just didn't want to make the trip and she was afraid to say no. I wish she had just said, "I would rather not do this," and I would have made another plan.

If your lips say yes when your heart says no, you are driving with your foot on the gas and brake at the same time. You will either nullify your efforts or lurch forward in jerking fits and starts. You would do far better to utter a full yes or a full no than to live at cross-purposes. The Bible tells us, "Let your yes be a yes, and your no be a no; everything else is the work of the devil." And what is the devil but action misaligned with intention?

Do not settle for half-hearted living. *Be total.* Be a compelling creator. If you act without your spirit fully engaged, you sabotage your results before you even begin. When you are fully present, you are powerful indeed! Successful people throw themselves into the task at hand. They know what they are here to do, capitalize on opportunities, and do not abandon their dreams when faced with a challenge. If you wish to attain that kind of mastery, your yes must be total, and so must your no.

How You Say Yes When You Mean No and What You Can Do

You Are Afraid People Will Not Like You If You Say No

A fellow in one of my seminars reported, "I was afraid to say no because I thought I would lose my friends if I did. But then I realized I didn't have any friends because no one knew who I was."

Honesty builds strong and reliable relationships. You win more by standing in your truth than by saying what is expected. Your friends and business associates with good sniffers will sense when you are withholding your truth and thus disconnected from your authentic power. "How can I trust your yes if I don't hear your no?"

If you sell yourself out to get approval, you will miss what you really want: *authenticity*, *passion*, and *aliveness*. When you say no to what does not match your intentions, you are saying yes to what you really want and you are one step closer to it. People with integrity will respect you more, not less, for following your truth. If people criticize or reject you for being authentic, do you really want to be with them? When you stand in your truth, you will find out who your true friends are. It is far better to have a few good friends who accept you for who you are than a lot of "friends" who accept you because you are doing the dance they expect. The only thing more important than people liking you is liking yourself. If you can "sleep in your own skin" at night, your life is a huge success.

You Try to Protect Others from Being Hurt

Many of us resist saying no because we do not want to reject someone or hurt their feelings. But we hurt them (and ourselves) more by acting as if something is working for us when it isn't. When you try to protect others, you are really seeking to protect yourself. If you trusted that your friends and associates were capable of handling your no—and helped by it—you would speak more truth. We diminish others by regarding them as weak and we affirm their strength when we communicate to them honestly.

My friend Dr. Carla Gordan was counseling a man who told her, "I have been married for over 30 years and the marriage is dead. My wife and I have nothing in common; we hardly talk and we live separate lives. I want very much to leave the marriage, but I cannot because she is too fragile and she could never take care of herself without me."

A month later Dr. Gordan was counseling a woman in another city. Her client reported, "My marriage is over and I have no reason to stay, except that my husband needs me and he would never survive if I left." As Carla spoke more with her client, she discovered the woman was married to the very man she had seen a month earlier! Both of them were unhappy, yet both were staying for the other person who did not want to be there.

If your connection is faltering for you, it is usually not working for the other person. I once hired a friend to work as my assistant. She flew to Hawaii from the Midwest and established her life on Maui. After a few weeks on the job, it became clear to me that her skills were not suited for the position. I felt in a quandary, since she had come so far and made so many significant life changes to work for me. I kept hesitating and trying to justify her staying in the position, but as time went on it became clear that this arrangement was not going to work. Finally I invited her out to lunch and planned to explain to her that I needed to get someone else for the job.

When we sat down at the restaurant, she told me, "I am glad we have this time together. There is something I want to talk to you about. I don't think this job is working out for me."

When I told her I was about to tell her the same thing, we had a good laugh. We both felt relieved. We had set out on the venture in good faith and no one was at fault; we just needed to do something else. She found another position for which she was better matched, and I hired another assistant who fulfilled the job description.

In relationships, unless everyone is winning, no one is winning. If your connection is faltering, don't linger in dissatisfaction. Either change the relationship or change your mind. You can usually find a way to upgrade the situation (or your attitude toward it) so everyone is taken care of. Often you can make changes within the situation, and sometimes you must move on. You can communicate anything, including leaving a job, relationship, or living situation, with love, appreciation, and respect. When I owned a rental property I occasionally had to give a tenant notice. Although I never liked doing this, I found that if I approached the person with kindness and honesty, the process would go smoothly, we would remain friends, and each of us would find a better match. If you offer someone sincerity and respect, you are protecting them in ways far deeper than avoiding saying no.

Rejection is protection. An honest no is as much a gift as an honest yes. It serves and blesses both giver and receiver. Behind every no is a yes. When you can find the yes, you will have the key to a win for everyone.

You Scatter Yourself

The greatest gift you can give others is your full presence. If you want to really succeed, *show up.* You have been taught that what you do is your contribution to life, while your deeper gift is *how you do it.* If you are going to do something, invest your full self. If you can't be there fully, don't be there at all. (How ripped-off do you feel when you are on the telephone saying something important to someone, and you hear them doing dishes, punching keys on their computer, or flushing the toilet?) When you act with resistance, resentment, or distraction, you poison your endeavor and relationship. (Paramahansa Yogananda noted, "Manners without sincerity are like a beautiful but dead lady.") If you find yourself doing something halfheartedly, stop and decide if you really want to do this; then either dive in or dive out.

Trying to do too many things at once is counterproductive and in some cases insulting. In a newspaper column I read a series of angry letters from supermarket clerks complaining about how rudely they are treated by customers talking on their cell phones in the checkout line. One clerk counted that out of over 200 people she served on her shift, 47 were talking on their cell phones. Most of them, she reported, were discourteous, acting as if she was interrupting them from something more important, while she was simply trying to help them. I believe these clerks' frustration was due not only to their customers' rudeness, but their energetic absence. As spiritual beings, we are nourished by our relationships, even when they are brief or passing. When we seek to connect with another person and they are not there, we are left feeling hungry. (Have you ever made love with someone who was not really present?) These clerks, already frustrated by the banality of their work, were reaching out for human contact, and when their customers treated them like an intrusion, they grew hurt and angry.

Cell phone conversations offer us many valuable lessons in being fully present. Trying to do two things at once results in neither getting done wholly. More and more countries and now states are banning the use of cell phones while driving. Some restaurants are prohibiting the use of cell phones in the dining area. (A survey in *Yahoo!* magazine [ironically, read by people who are technologically well-wired] reports that 63 percent of respondents favored a prohibition of cell phone use in restaurants.) If you have ever sat down to enjoy a meal and heard a businessman a few feet away conducting a deal in a loud voice, you know how disturbing this can be. If you are going to eat, sit down and enjoy your meal. If you are going to do a deal, really do it. Trying to do both at the same time doesn't double your pleasure; it diminishes it. Are you here to do as much as you can, or be as much as you can?

You Don't Set Healthy Boundaries

Your actions speak your yes or no even more emphatically than your words. If you let things happen that you don't want to happen, you are saying yes while meaning no. If you do not set healthy boundaries, you cannot blame others for intruding on you. You are not a victim. You just didn't say no when you should have. Draw your lines well and your life will be your own.

I used to have a hard time saying no until I became known through my books and seminars. Then, as my public profile grew, more people wanted things from me. They wanted endorsements, publication of their book, connections to influential friends of mine, space to promote their products in my seminars and newsletters, counseling, loans and contributions, jobs, career advice, debate, travel suggestions, sex, marriage, attention, and all kinds of other things. There was nothing wrong with these folks wanting these things, and I don't blame them for asking; I just could not fulfill them. So I had to learn to lovingly say no to more things than I said yes to. (Sometimes I wonder if I stepped into this position so I could learn to say no!)

Here are some key areas in which you can practice setting healthy boundaries:

Time

Decide how much time you are going to devote to a person, meeting, or project, and then stick to it; show up when you say you will, leave when you say you will, and ask others to do the same.

Personal Physical Space

Create your own nurturing space and be vigilant about who you allow into it. If you like visitors showing up anytime unannounced, that is fine. If not, claim your right to your personal haven. If you spend lots of time mingling in other arenas, your period of self-renewal will make you more effective when you venture forth again. Make the décor and energy in your personal space an expression of your values and choices.

Money

Use your money for your true intentions rather than the demands of others. Decide how much you are willing to invest in a person or project and remain firm. Before lending or borrowing, give the prospect considerable thought and be sure you are doing it with a whole heart. If your choice is to invest, lend, or donate, proceed full steam ahead. Act out of choice, not guilt. Let it be okay to not give if your inner guidance so speaks to you. Earmark what you want to use your money for *before* it comes in. If you have a challenge with credit cards, cut them up or set clear spending limits. If you practice tithing, stay with it no matter what. Set aside some money for fun and don't retract your commitment to self-nurturing.

Work

Your career is not supposed to be a drudgery, but an avenue for creative self-expression. Decide how much you want to work in the course of a day or a week. Tell your boss when you are available and when you are not. At home, screen your calls or shut your phone off during the hours you do not want to be reached. When you make a social or recreational appointment, keep it even if work beckons. Cut away the aspects of your work that drag you down, and expand the elements that bring you life. Read *The Man Who Mistook His Job for a Life* by Jonathon Lazear. Let your passion guide your vocation.

Sex

Have sex with the person you choose, when you choose, and how you choose. Sex at any level less than joyful self-expression and mutual caring will tatter your soul. Be up-front about your choices regarding birth control, sexual health protection, and kinky explorations. Sex is *not* the area of life to be polite; it requires total authenticity. If your sex life is tainted with a sense of upset, obligation, or duress, you cannot really call it making love. Once your intentions are clear and your heart is open, let loose and swing for the bleachers.

Emotional Availability

Be emotionally supportive to your friends, loved ones, and clients, but stop when you start to feel drained. Some people will take as much time and energy as you are willing to give (like *all* of it). Be present and helpful, but not to the extent that your interaction undermines your life force. Some people don't even care who you are or if you are listening; they don't even care if you are *alive*. They just want to talk, and another body in the room or on the other end of the telephone line makes them feel like they are accomplishing something. They are not. They are emotional necrophiliacs, and would probably get as much reward delivering their story to a corpse. If you listen long enough, you will become one. Help them and yourself by not feeding their addiction. Just love them and be where you are supposed to be. Sometimes the kindest gift you can offer to someone who needs to stand on their own feet is a kind refusal to play a crutch.

Spiritual Practice

The most important boundary you can set is the time to nourish your spirit. The few minutes a day you take to feed your soul is your strongest investment in your happiness. Do whatever it takes to inspire yourself and stay in a creative consciousness. Choose a time each day to connect with your inner being and do not compromise it. Consider it non-negotiable. People who truly love you will understand and support you to do it. Anyone who chastises you for your self-care practice or demands your attention instead of it is clearly out of tune with your destiny and should be released to find theirs.

One more note on boundary setting: Running away is not a healthy form of boundary setting. It is a form of running away. I know a couple who allowed the husband's sister to move in with them temporarily, which turned into permanently. Neither of the couple could find the courage to ask her to leave, so they bought a new house and left the sister in the old one. But then the sister cried and they took her with them to the new home. Then they ended up with two mortgages and an uninvited sister. If they had just asked her to leave, they would have saved themselves a lot of hassles. The "easy" way turned out to be the hard way.

You Participate in Relationships Where You Don't Belong

Staying in a relationship where you don't want to be is a disservice to your partner and yourself. It may seem kinder to stay, but it is actually crueler. This principle applies not just to romantic relationships, but to friendships, family, and business associations. Yes, it may be difficult to let go, but after a point it becomes more of a struggle to hold on. As the song goes, you have to know "when to hold 'em and know when to fold 'em."

Leaving a relationship does not always mean you must go away. Sometimes your boredom, pain, or conflict is an invitation to move to the next level with your partner. In this sense, you are being called to leave a relationship that is not working and recreate it so it matches your vision.

Romantic Relationships

If you have left or know you are going to leave; or if someone has left you or they are not really with you, don't prolong the agony. Cut the cord. Do it lovingly, but do it firmly. Hovering in a twilight zone is excruciating. Why torture yourself or your partner? Dive in or dive out, but don't stand by the side of the pool with your teeth chattering.

Toxic Relationships

Some relationships are downright abusive, and no one with any self-respect should be subject to them. If your partner regularly hurts you physically, emotionally, or mentally, get out while you are still alive. This also applies to family members who dump guilt habitually; businesses in which an employer (or employee) makes unreasonable demands; and friendships in which one person takes advantage of another. Your mind chides, "You deserve to put up with this," while your soul urges you, "Take care of yourself." Listen to the voice of reason, not guilt or fear.

Mismatched Relationships

You may find yourself working, living, or sleeping with someone who does not share your values or intentions. Their interests may be honorable, but they do not match yours. If your differences are minor, you can overlook them. But if you are watching significantly different movies, there is no purpose in trying to force the situation. No one is wrong. You just both have a right place elsewhere.

Dead Relationships

Numerous times I have renewed contact with friends from my past, some as far back as grade school and high school. After the initial excitement of re-connecting, going over stories of graduation night, and catching up on what our old friends are doing, we have nothing left to talk about. We try to find things in common, but there is not much there. We have grown in different directions and lead different lives. We are not the same people that we were 20 years ago. While part of me wants to resurrect the good old days, we cannot. Those days were good because of who we were then. There are other good things about these days. If you find yourself in such a situation, simply enjoy what you have to talk about, and don't try to push for more. If this person has a place in your life now, you will know it; if not, you can simply appreciate who you and your friends were then, and stay with what brings you life now.

You Procrastinate

Wait! Don't put this section off until later!

The propensity to put things off until later often stems from reluctance to say no now. If, when presented with a request or invitation, you are not sure what to do, by all means wait until you know. But if you know that you are not going to do it, help the person making the request by saying no now. Otherwise they will hold your non-response as a possible yes, even while you are thinking no. The longer you wait to respond, the harder it will be. Clean up your relationships by giving clear responses as soon as you know them, especially when the answer is no.

You Second Guess Yourself

Continuing to go back and forth after you've made a decision is even more excruciating than saying yes while meaning no. If you have already said yes, then go with it, and do the same for no. Often it does not matter *what* you decide; it just matters that you *do* decide. The universe will rally around any decision you make; be sure you are rallying with it. *Your decisions are honorable because they are your own.* You can make any decision work if you believe in it. If the results of your decisions suck, you may not have made bad decisions; you might just be doubting yourself. You are either criticizing your choice now or you did not heed your inner voice when you first chose. Second-guessing yourself is a sort of postpartum procrastination. If you sit in the middle of the road, you will get hit by traffic moving in both directions. Quit mind-screwing yourself and give your creations the support they deserve.

You Say Yes When You Mean Maybe

"Maybe" is not a "yes." If you feel maybe, don't say yes. Say maybe. If you're not sure, sit with your decision until you are sure. The process will keep bubbling inside you until you get clear. At some point you will know, and you will be glad you waited until you were sure. If, for example, you are shopping and you see an item you like but you are not sure if you want it, leave it be. Then, if it keeps calling to you, go back and get it. If you forget about it, it wasn't for you.

Confusion is a very powerful position to work from; it signifies you are on the verge of a breakthrough. Your old beliefs or conditions (usually limited) are bumping up against new and greater possibilities. When you are confused, you are not stalled; you are gathering data. Even if you think you are making no progress, be assured that things are developing within you, and they will make perfect sense when they reach the surface. "Sweating the opposites" will move you to a new depth of knowing and stronger-than-ever choice. If you are not sure what to do, don't just do something—stand there. Don't make a decision just because you think you have to decide now. Wait until you know. Then, when you do choose, you will know why. Your yes will be a real yes. Don't complain about being confused—milk it.

You Say No When You Mean Yes

Saying no to what you do want is the same as saying yes to what you don't want. It is a sellout. Whenever you do not honor your inner truth, you get jumbled up inside until you go back and express the truth you stifled.

We deny our desires for dysfunctional reasons: guilt; a sense of unworthiness; fear of success; desire to appear unselfish; resistance to move beyond a familiar self-image or lifestyle; self-sabotage; and peer or family pressure. Don't waste a moment analyzing or justifying your motivation. If your heart pulls you in a direction, heed its joy as soon as you know it. Life is unlimited in its ability to support you. When you become unlimited in your willingness to support yourself, you will receive all that life has to offer.

You Don't Say No to Your Kids

Your children need limits as much as love. Limits are *a form* of love. If you fear saying no to your children (or students or clients), they will not know how to say no to themselves when they need to. Remember that every no is a yes to something else; keep in mind what that yes is, and the no will make sense. I once dated someone who had a very unruly child. The boy threw tantrums wherever he went and became physically destructive.

When I asked his mother why she let him do whatever he wanted, she told me that she wanted him to be free. But he was not free; if a situation arose in which he needed to not throw a tantrum, he did not have an option.

If you respect your no, so will your kids. Your difficulty in saying no is not about them; it is about you. When you believe in your healthy boundaries and honor them, so will your children.

Yes and no are two sides of one coin. Invest it where you like. You don't just have a right to be where you choose with whom you choose—you have a responsibility. That is the only way your life will match your dreams. You can recreate your entire life to be a delicious expression of your heart's desires. But you must first make a stand for your intentions. You have underestimated the power and importance of your honest no. Now it is time to make it your friend.

YOU THINK YOU HAVE TO DO IT ALL *Yourself*

In the garden of the Sarasota, Florida estate of fabled circus entrepreneur John Ringling stands an impressive bronze statue of the Roman god Atlas bearing the world on his shoulders. The first thing I noticed about Atlas was that he was not a happy camper. Atlas was struggling dreadfully and appeared to be on the verge of caving in. Dude, carrying the weight of the world is overbearing.

While Atlas is often romanticized, his job sucks. If you accept his position, your life will suck. If you assume responsibility for everyone and everything around you, you will rapidly become a crispy critter. Besides, it doesn't work. When you try to run the whole show, you get frazzled, frayed, and fatigued. You feel overwhelmed, grow resentful, and then lash out inappropriately, blowing little things into major issues. Over time you may become ill. Shoulder pain, stomach problems, and high blood pressure are strong indicators that you are trying to play Atlas.

If you examine your responsibilities more closely, you will discover it is not the universe that has piled too much on your plate. It is you. You have taken on jobs not assigned to you. You are trying too hard. Frustration and conflict are messages from the universe that it is time to back off. The longer you wait to get the message, the harder your journey will be. Let go now and beat the rush later.

If you are a control freak (or you are dealing with one), your issue is not power; it is trust. If you think you have to do it all, you don't trust anyone else to help. You don't have faith in others' ability to meet your standards. "Nothing gets done right unless I do it," is your weighty mantra. But if you never let people be strong enough to support you, how will you ever find anyone who can?

The people in your world will be as big—or small—as you let them be. Their attitudes and abilities are not absolute hard facts. Your expectations play a major role in how they perform. You have probably seen children act ornery and irresponsible with one parent, yet helpful and cooperative with another parent or friend. Or perhaps you have been in the middle of an argument with your relationship partner when the phone rings. She picks up the phone, is pleased to hear the voice of a friend, and spends several minutes chatting amiable, even laughing. Then she hangs up and returns to you with a vengeance. What's up with that? Different people draw forth different aspects from each other. You can shape the behavior of others by means of the image you hold of them. Appreciate their talents and they will come forth. Expect them to be incompetent, and you will have good reason to have to do it all yourself.

Yet behind your underestimation of others brews an even more crucial issue: *You don't trust life.* Albert Einstein stated, "All scientific inquiry seeks to answer one fundamental question: *Is the universe a friendly place?*" If it isn't, you are fully justified in feverishly trying to control everyone and everything that threatens you. You might as well put this book down right now and go out and buy infrared binoculars, rifles, and survival food supplies. Satan is on a campaign to ravage your good and he will surely snatch your joy the moment you let your guard down. And above all else, don't let anyone into your heart—it's been broken too many times to be vulnerable again.

But if there is an intelligent force for good operating behind the events in your life, you can relax. You can take the energy you have been using to keep the world from falling apart and rechannel it into creative expression. You can quit defending yourself from people who might hurt you, and enjoy people who might love you. You can laugh about things that once seemed painful, and find gifts in events you once considered overwhelming. You can quit sweating to make sure nothing goes wrong, and appreciate the many things that are going right.

More help is available than you realize. Independence is good, but if you are drowning in responsibilities, you have assumed more than your share. We are interdependent. We need each other. And we have each other.

HOW YOU THINK YOU HAVE TO DO IT ALL YOURSELF AND WHAT YOU CAN DO

You Think Everything Depends on You

If you think the world will fall apart if you do not keep it together, your ego has swallowed Viagara and you need to cool out. Yes, you are responsible for your domain; no, your domain does not extend to Jupiter. Yes, you need to take care of the tasks before you; no, you do not need to take care of the tasks before others. Yes, you have an effect on your children; no, they are not stupid. They are quite smart, and they will either make good choices or learn from their errors. If you try to manage their choices, you deprive them of their right and power to build wisdom muscles as they go. (Besides, they will ultimately do what they want, anyway.) The world survived long before you showed up and it will survive long after you are gone. If you want to make the world a better place, let life flow. A poignant Zen aphorism notes, "Sitting quietly, doing nothing, spring comes and the grass grows."

I attended a friend's birthday party at a local beach. My friend's mother attended, and she decided she would make sure everyone had a good time. (You can see where this is headed.) From the moment the guests arrived, the mother orchestrated where everyone was to sit, how far apart their blankets were to be, how and where the food was to be put out, when people were to eat, and on and on. While she was trying to be helpful, her nervous energy was irritating and detracted from the natural flow of the event. The guests could figure out where to sit; it didn't really matter how far their blankets were apart; and when they got hungry, they would find their way to the food. Most of us had been eating for our entire lives, and finding food at a party posed no big existential dilemma. I'm sure mom was having the least fun of everyone there.

If you think the world would unravel if you did not keep it glued, lay back more. Watch what happens when you allow life to take care of itself. If there is something you really need to do, you will know it. If not, don't try to solve problems before they occur. In so doing, you create all kinds of problems that wouldn't have happened if you weren't trying to head them off.

You Refuse to Accept Help

Many of us (especially men) were taught that asking for help is a sign of weakness; it is nobler to die trying alone than to reach out for support. This, of course, is ka-ka. Have you ever wrestled for hours or days with a software problem or a knock in your car engine, when you could have simply picked up the telephone and called technical support or taken the car to a mechanic? Sure, there is satisfaction in figuring out how to fix stuff, but when it becomes an obsession, you lose more than you gain.

Face it: nobody knows how to do everything. Nobody has time to do everything. Nobody is supposed to do everything. Nobody *wants* to do everything. Our society, economy, and relationships work best when everyone contributes their unique talents and skills. If you don't let others contribute to you, you mess up the system—mostly for yourself. Sure, you can have sex with yourself, but wouldn't you rather have a partner? (This is *not* the time to apply the aphorism, "The helping hand you have been seeking is at the end of your own arm.")

When you allow others to assist you, you bestow a great gift to them. Imagine they would actually *like* to help you. Imagine they actually *can* help you. Imagine they would still *respect* you—maybe *more)* if you let them be there for you. If you are always the helper and never the *helpee*, you cut yourself off from the great circulation of life. You are hiding behind your role as giver. Accepting support is a sign of strength and maturity. Receiving help does not mean you are defective; it means you are a real person. Get over the "I don't need your help" thing. It is hurting you more than you realize. Being helpable feels really good—and it *works*.

You Resist Delegating

Mothers, managers, and small business owners, get out your highlighter. If you resist delegating, you end up doing all kinds of things you don't want or need to do. Then you wonder why you feel overwhelmed. Or why your business isn't growing. Or why your children are so needy. It's not them. It's you.

Your way out is simple, but not easy: Admit that there are other people in the universe who can do some things as well as you. Maybe—hold onto your seat, now—even *better* than you. I know this is a totally radical, unreasonable, and heretical concept to suggest, but alas, it may be so.

Letting other people take over some of the things you are doing, alien as this sounds, offers some very attractive benefits: 1) You can quit doing things you don't want to do; 2) You free yourself to do the things you want to do; 3) Your business's productivity and income will increase; 4) You will support and empower others to develop their gifts and talents and be rewarded for them; 5) Everyone will be happier and healthier; and 6) You might actually have a life.

Very successful people are good delegators. Take Bill Gates, for example, the richest man in America. Bill Gates makes executive decisions and then lets thousands of people implement them. If he tried to do their jobs, he would not have the time or focus to be a visionary leader. He knows what his time and energy are worth. (You can log onto the Internet and find many Websites tracking Bill Gates's wealth. Numerous people have nothing better to do than sit around and count his money. I'm sure they spend more time thinking about how rich Bill is than he does.) If Bill Gates was walking down a hall at Microsoft and he saw a $1,000 bill lying on the floor, *it would not be worth his time* to bend over and pick it up. In the same amount of time it would take Bill to pick up the bill, he is earning more money by doing what he does. Bill Gates is true to his talents and he lets others be true to theirs.

Your time is valuable, too, and your activities should be commensurate with your worth. If you earn $50,000 a year, for example, that translates to almost $32 an hour. If you are performing any aspect of your business that you could hire someone else to do for less than $32 an hour, you are losing money by doing those things. Like stapling booklets, vacuuming the rug, or returning unimportant calls. Make a list of all the things you like to do and the things you don't like to do, and then hire someone to do the things you don't want to do. ("If it's not fun, hire it done.") If you both do your job properly, your business will earn enough money to pay your assistant's salary and increase your income as well. And you'll both enjoy yourselves . . . who would have thought?

You Have to Always Be Right

If this suggestion bothers you, it applies to you. The need to always be right is the progeny of an antiquated patriarchal mentality relying on bravado to disguise insecurity. In other words, anyone who needs to always be right is a wimp. Many rigid people die from stress-related diseases because they'd rather be right than happy. Like the guy who was about to pass through a green light at an intersection when he saw another car about to run the red light. He had the right of way, so he just kept going. Both drivers got killed—but the important thing is that he was *right*.

One evening I brought a video home to watch with my partner. When I inserted the cassette into the VCR, all we saw on the screen was snow. "Maybe you should run the head cleaner," she suggested.

"That can't be it," I told her. "If the head was dirty, we'd see some picture. One of these connections must be messed up." I began to fuss with the wires and buttons.

Several minutes later she asked, "Why don't you just try the head cleaner?"

I began to feel annoyed. She didn't know anything about electronics, and I did. "Just give me a minute," I answered. "I'll fix it."

A few more minutes went by and I made no progress. Then she tapped me on the shoulder and handed me the head cleaner. "I think it might work," she stated soberly.

By this time I was pretty worked up and I was getting tired of her silly suggestion. So I decided to just get her off my case.

I would run the head cleaner, she would see it didn't work, and I could get on with the real business of fixing the machine.

I put the head cleaner through its cycle and *voilà*—instant picture. Oops. Although I was sure I was right, I was wrong. Thinking about the scenario later, I was glad I was wrong. If I was right, we never would have gotten to see the movie that night.

Lots of times you are right, and sometimes you are not. If you have to be right, you are automatically wrong. It takes a big person to step off their position and listen to someone else's viewpoint. But if your commitment to success is greater than your need to be right, you will win—not at another's expense, but along with them.

You Won't Let Anyone into Your Heart

Everyone has experienced a broken heart. Most of us have at some time thought or said, "I will never love again." In the wake of emotional pain, it is natural to want to protect yourself. And in many situations it's a good idea to retreat into a cocoon for a period of time while you regroup.

The problem is that when you keep your heart sheltered, you do not emerge from the cocoon. You end up as a sleeping caterpillar and never enjoy the exhilarating flight of the butterfly. In your self-protection you numb yourself to your passion, which is the key to the happiness you seek. You did not find love by giving yourself away, but neither will you find it by hiding. You were not born to live in the cold and dark. You were born to know the love you seek.

There are two ways you can respond to a broken heart: 1) Stop loving; or 2) Love more.

If your heart has been broken,
let it be broken open.

Do not use your breakup or betrayal as an excuse to shut down your heart; instead, practice loving more, beginning with yourself. Praise yourself for the strides you made rather than condemning yourself for your errors. Appreciate your partner for their contribution to your life rather than crucifying them for what they took away. They do not have the power to take away your good; only you can remove it by pandering to fear. And only you can restore it by generating the love you thought you needed from someone else. Your former partner assisted you to learn a major lesson in loving: *you cannot afford to stop*. When you turn off the faucet of your joy, you are the one who loses. And when you keep it open, you win big time. Use every experience as rocket fuel to take you where you want to go.

*Take what you have
and make what you want.*

It doesn't matter what avenue through which you let love into your life; you can practice on anyone or anything. In a seminar I led, I discovered a common theme among the participants: they had all shut down on people, but had great relationships with their pets. They found their relationships with their dogs, cats, birds, and horses safer than relationships with people. It makes perfect sense. Animals, especially dogs, lavish upon us unconditional love, for which we deeply long. A study showed that when patients in several nursing homes were allowed to keep small lap pets, their medication need was reduced by 70 percent and their mortality rate slowed by 50 percent. It is not medication that keeps us alive or lack of it that kills us. It is giving and receiving love that sustains us.

When you have learned the power of love from your pet, work yourself up to a human being. Certainly people are more complex, yet the principles of loving are the same. Just think of your man as a big Golden Retriever or your woman as a saucy Lhasa Apso. Feed them good stuff, take them out to play, scratch their belly regularly, and tell them how wonderful they are. Don't keep their collar too tight or their leash too short. Don't beat them (with words) to get what you want; they will only become paranoid and turn on you or run away. When mating, just go with your natural instincts. Everybody innately knows how to mate, and if you don't stifle yourself with other people's opinions, you will have a bunch of fun.

Loving another person is a gift you give yourself. The love you give flows through you, so no matter how they respond, you receive the benefit of loving. True love never requires a response. If you are frustrated because you are not being loved in return, you are not really loving. Be a lover and you will find all the love you seek. As D.H. Lawrence eloquently noted,

Those who go searching for love
only find their own lovelessness.
But the loveless never find love;
only the loving find love,
And they never have to search for it.

You Do Not Make Use of Your Higher Power

There is an intelligent power operating behind the scenes of life. If you latch hold of it, you have all the help you need to do anything you choose. With this power you can move mountains. Without it, you feel lost, alone, confused, and alienated.

Our entire society functions by way of invisible forces. No one has ever seen electricity, yet our business and personal lives depend on it. You start your car from a battery, nuke your lunch with a microwave, and watch television via a satellite beaming unseen signals from hundreds of miles in space. Your dental hygienist peers into the center of your teeth with x-rays and then cleans them with ultrasound vibrations. You communicate through telephone and e-mail, then surf the Internet via countless energy blips bouncing around the globe. Inside your computer zillions of imperceptible sparks dance at lightning speed around a miniscule circuit board. IBM recently announced the invention of a nanocarbon microchip that will run the computers of tomorrow. This microchip is 100,000 times smaller than a human hair, and functions at a *molecular* level. The part of the computer that you see is the least integral of the equipment. All of the important actions operate behind the scenes.

The principle of "The Force" was woven by producer George Lucas into the *Star Wars* film series. And a brilliant concept it is! Just before the release of the much-anticipated *Episode One,* leading actor Liam Neeson recounted a conversation in an interview in *Premiere* Magazine:

> *Here it is as George Lucas explained it to me . . . In our bodies we have thousands of different strains of bacteria. What if one of those strains has an intelligence that is in communication with the energy of the universe? All the energy, all the stuff to which you give names like Buddha and God—that's the capability of the Jedi.*

Within you at this moment is a pipeline to infinite wisdom, power, and love. A part of your mind is always aware of your passion, purpose, and identity. If you do not believe this wisdom exists or if you do not seek to access it, you will not enjoy its benefits. If you consciously open to it and cultivate your connection with it, you will find all the help you need from a mighty unseen hand.

I spoke with a successful and well-respected business consultant who works closely with people at all levels of the corporate world. I asked him if he had discovered any characteristics that successful business leaders have in common.

"Yes," he answered. "The higher up the corporate ladder you go, the more people acknowledge a spiritual source. CEO's talk more freely about a higher power than anyone else." He went on to explain, "Executives don't make it to the top of their company by doing it all themselves. Eventually they recognize they need help. When they open to work in partnership with a higher power, their lives and careers take off."

What you call this higher power is not important; what is important is that you develop a relationship with it. Many call this higher power, "God." Unfortunately, the word "God" has been ravaged by religious abuse. Many people shut down the moment they hear the word "God" because they have learned to associate the name with fear, oppressive judgment, and divisiveness. The word creates as many blocks to communication as bridges. I have a very deep appreciation for a God of love. Yet I have discovered that when I utter the word during a lecture, many people in the audience have their hackles go up because as children they were taught they were deficient or evil and God was going to punish them. So I and others have had to find a new vocabulary to express the same truth in ways that will invite people to relax and listen rather than retreat to knee-jerk reaction. Words like *Spirit, Higher Power, Source Energy, Life-force, Essence, Universal Mind, Inner Being,* and *Higher Self* all work well. Or, if you like, "Ethel" or "Abdul." God doesn't care what you call It. God just cares about the sincerity of your heart. People fight over whose name of God is the right one. They are severely deluded. Sanity recognizes that God is love, and all else is details.

During the 1980s I made three citizen diplomacy journeys to the Soviet Union. The Cold War had been going on for 30 years and showed little sign of easing. People got tired of waiting for the government to make peace, so we decided to do it ourselves. (We fulfilled President Eisenhower's prophecy that "One day the people of the world will want peace so much that the governments will have to get out of their way and let them have it.") Many groups like mine traveled to the U.S.S.R.

to build person-to-person bridges of friendship, love, and understanding.

We were thrilled to find the Russians were wonderful people, and very much like ourselves. They cherished their lives and their children, and they were just as fearful of war as we were. I could write an entire book recounting the extraordinary relationships we developed with the Russian people; each time I journeyed there, my life changed in a huge way.

During one open forum with a Soviet media representative, a member of our group challenged him about the Soviet philosophy of Atheism. "Do you not accept the reality of a higher power?" our member asked. The Soviet answered, "We believe in a power that lives within us." Our group members looked at each other, astonished. "That's what we believe, too," we acknowledged.

We found the Russians to be a deeply spiritual people with a great deal of faith and heart. The Atheism purported by Communism bore no relation to the people; it was strictly a government ideology. Citizens mouthed the words because they were forced to, but behind closed doors they expressed and embodied lofty spiritual values. I learned that we can invent all kinds of worldly philosophies devoid of spirit, but, like tiny blades of grass that find their way through cement and eventually dislodge it, sooner or later our spiritual nature shines through.

Every great spiritual teacher has acknowledged a higher power as their source and the headwaters of all good. In the beloved Twenty-third Psalm, King David poetically extolled, "The Lord is my Shepherd; I shall not want." Lao Tsu, author of the immortal *Tao Te Ching*, observed, "Through the Tao all things are done. If powerful men and women could center themselves in it, the whole world would be transformed." Buddha spoke time and again of the importance of self-emptying. Jesus took no personal credit for the healings he performed. He declared, "It is not I, but the Father within me who does the work." Later Albert Einstein, one of the most brilliant scientists of all time, noted, "My religion consists of a humble admiration of the illimitable superior spirit who reveals himself in the slight details we are able to perceive with our frail and feeble mind."

Whether or not you are religious doesn't matter. What is important is that you recognize a higher reality that supercedes the illusions that frighten you. That reality is present in you, through you, and around you. Take any scary situation, hold it up to love, and the tentacles of fear lose their icy grip. *"Fear knocked at the door. Faith answered, and no one was there."*

Loneliness in all its forms springs from the belief you must do it all yourself. When you feel abandoned, life can get very scary; when you feel connected, you proceed with the confidence of kings. *A Course in Miracles* tells us, "If you knew who walks beside you, fear would be impossible." Whether you believe in God, love, people, science, or your pooch, one thing is certain: *You have help.* The intelligent resourceful universe keeps showing up to support those who need it— sometimes in miraculous ways. A woman told me that she had wanted to come to Hawaii for a seminar, but didn't have the funds for airfare. She figured that if she could not come to be in my program, she would read one of my books that she had had for a while. She went to her bookshelf, opened the book, and out fell a check someone had given her a year earlier. It was in the amount of $450—exactly what she needed for the airfare.

Such an experience is not a fluke; it is a demonstration of how universal principles get behind you as you align with them. Miracles do not suspend the laws of life; they fulfill them. The river of life is always flowing; your part is to get your boat into the water and let the current power you. It's all a lot easier than you've been told. Give Atlas a break; he's ready.

YOU TRY TO FIX OTHER
People

My mother's goal in life was to feed me. Mom was a Jewish mother—what do you expect? Most of the time, I liked being fed. The problem came when I wasn't hungry and she tried to feed me anyway. Once, after I was grown and living on my own, I went to visit her. She offered to make me a salad, and I accepted. Mom sat down at the kitchen table with me and presented me with an attractive bowl of greens. Then she took a tomato and knife and began to cut the tomato into the salad, slice by slice. "Say 'When,'" she told me. After a few slices I said, "When." But that didn't stop her. "When," I repeated. She started to cut faster. "When!" I practically yelled as I pulled the plate out from under her, toward me. Then she not only cut faster and harder, she followed the plate around the table, trying to get as many tomatoes into my bowl as she could before I snatched it away. God love her.

If you ignore other people's "when," you're just wasting your tomatoes. If you try to cut them when they haven't even requested them, you're wasting more of your tomatoes. And if you keep cutting when they have spelled out to you that they don't want them, you're wasting all of your tomatoes.

While most people want to be helpful, sometimes what is disguised as help is not help at all. It is more to meet the need or alleviate the discomfort of the giver than the receiver. In such a case no giving really happens; to the contrary, the situation becomes more mucky and it undermines the potential healing relationship between giver and receiver.

If you ever feel motivated to fix someone, here is a word of advice: *Save your tomatoes.* Face it: Nothing is more annoying to you than someone who tries to change you or coerce you to their way of thinking. Ultimately you become only more defiant. Why would you expect someone else to respond otherwise? No one wants to be fixed. They just want to be loved. No one wants to be labeled. They just want to be appreciated. No one wants to be seen as defective. They just want to be whole. When you appreciate people for who they are, you create an ideal environment for them to grow. When you focus on their positive qualities and emphasize their talents, they will feel so accepted and empowered that their dysfunctions will have no reinforcement, and melt away naturally. Advice, pressure, and punishment do not heal. The great healer is love.

Trying to fix others is a long, frustrating, and ultimately losing battle. You will never succeed because you began with three false premises: 1) There is something wrong with them; 2) You know what their problem is and how they should be living instead; and 3) You have the right and power to choose for them or to force them to make the choices you think they should make.

It seems easier to try to change others than to face yourself. Yet it is not your purpose to repair another person. Your purpose is to wake up. You need not fix yourself because you are not broken, and you need not fix others because they are not broken. Your idea of who they are is broken. Rather than trying to change them, upgrade your vision. Ironically, when you regard them as whole, no matter what appearances indicate, you are in a perfect position to influence them toward positive change.

The Indian sage Ramana Maharshi taught one simple method of enlightenment: Keep asking, "Who am I?" If you ask this question continuously and sincerely, you will peel away the false identities you have adopted—always smaller than your true self—and reveal your true inner splendor. Ramana posed an incisive question: "Do all the characters in your dream have to wake up before you can wake up?" Your awakening does not depend on the actors in your dream; the moment you awaken, the entire dream, no matter how horrible, dissolves, and all of the actors are liberated along with you.

To think you know what is best for another person is an industrial-strength ego trip. When you try to play God, you overlook that God is playing your friend. From your limited human perspective, you cannot understand all the factors why someone exhibits a certain behavior; why and on what level they have chosen it; its relation to their life purpose; what they are learning from it; where it is ultimately leading them; and how it fits into the choices and lessons of others with whom they interact. All you see is one little piece in a multi-billion-piece jigsaw, and it would be presumptuous and preposterous to imagine you see the whole puzzle.

If you could fix someone, you would rob them of free choice, which morally sucks. Free choice means that everyone has the right to live in heaven, hell, or Chicago, and they also have the right to move. They are free to take on challenges and then build the muscles to overcome them, which is why the difficulty arose in the first place. On an airplane I sat next to a woman who works for the U.S. Army. She trains soldiers to go into toxic environments and stay alive. In one of the exercises, she sends soldiers into a room filled with poison gas. There someone removes their gas mask and she assesses what they do under pressure. Some soldiers do well and others panic. Then she takes the soldiers who panic and either trains them to handle the challenge, or releases them from the program. From the momentary perspective of an outside observer, it would seem that taking their gas mask for a few minutes is cruel. But when you step back and consider the big picture, she is helping them learn a skill that could save their lives and enable them to save the lives of others. So before you can decide what is truly helpful, you have to know all the facts. We rarely do.

If you had the right and power to choose for others, they would have the right and power to choose for you. That would totally suck. Then you would have to marry the person your mother decides is best for you, jump like a flea to your boss's every whim, and sit through long slide shows of your brother-in-law's Moose convention. If this sounds distasteful, afford your friends and loved ones the same respect you would wish for yourself.

But what about really helping others? What if someone asks you for help, or needs it without knowing it? What if someone wants to just sit and watch *Baywatch* reruns for the rest of their life and needs an intervention? What if your best friend is sporting a Godzilla-size booger on her way to a big date? Would it not be kinder to tell her?

Here's a simple rule for helping:

> *If you are upset about their problem,*
> *it's your problem. If you are not upset,*
> *you are in a perfect position to help.*

Your upset over someone else's behavior is a signal for you rather than them. You have a charge on the issue because you have not come to terms with it yourself. The behavior either reminds you of something about yourself you dislike, or something someone has done in the past you have not come to terms with. (I dated someone who told me she did not like the way I breathed because it reminded her of a former boyfriend she didn't like—what's a guy to do?) When you are wigged out by someone else's behavior, you are in the *least* optimal position to change them. Instead—and I know it's really hard—do your best to step back and get your head on straight. Break the momentum of your impulse to get in their face. Then, a few minutes, hours, or days later, when you feel more centered, if you still feel moved to approach them, do so from that position. The results will be infinitely more rewarding for both of you. If you jump all over them with anger or upset, you will hook them and elicit a defensive reaction. Then you will not be helpful at all. To the contrary, you will probably argue and go your separate ways mad.

It is really rare and practically unheard of (unless the recipient of your criticism has worked in a complaint department), that someone will respond to a dump with poise and aplomb. Don't expect them to field a barrage gracefully. If you really want this situation resolved, get centered *before* you approach them and bring them the benefit of your conscious perspective. Jesus offered a penetrating analogy: Do not try to remove the speck from your friend's eye while you have a huge log in your own. First remove the log and then go to your friend to remove the speck. This is not simply a religious teaching; it is master psychology.

If someone asks you for help, serving them takes on an entirely different dynamic than trying to fix them. If a friend comes to you and asks, "Can you show me how to rollerblade?" or "Do you have any feedback for me on the talk I just gave?" or "Is everything all right between us?" you are being offered an open door. In such a case your response will be valued and heard, for you will be expressing from a position of clarity and service. You will not be trying to fix, but assist. And your results will be far more effective.

A Course in Miracles suggests that before you enter into any situation calling for teaching, healing, or human relations, remind yourself, *"I am here only to be truly helpful."* The operative word here is *truly*. What would real help look like in this moment? Ask yourself, "What does this person need to receive?" rather than "What do I want to give?" Real help is never about imposing your will on others. It is about offering them a conducive atmosphere in which to grow. You can't pry the petals of a flower open, but you can provide the flower with healthy soil and plenty of sunlight and water. Then, when the petals do blossom, they will unfold in just the right way and time, and the flower will be an expression of beauty and grace.

Is there ever a situation in which you must snatch someone away from a precipice they are about to drive over? Yes, but much more rarely than you think. If there is absolutely no question in your mind (like sitting in the passenger seat with someone who is driving drunk, or discovering that someone is abusing a child) that you have to do something, do it. But such situations are exceptional. Most of the time trusting, relaxing, and supporting are in order.

Assuming the position of General Manager of the Universe is a thankless task that will not alleviate hardship in your life, but only aggravate it. I have counseled many people who have taken on the job (we can't *all* be the one), and I can assure you the mission is booby-trapped. Your efforts will not take you where you really want to go. As I have released myself from having to fix others, my life has become much lighter and freer. I feel better, get along with others more fluently, and achieve far more effective results. When you regard others as empowered souls rather than broken toys, they are much more likely to stand on their own and be happy. Along with you.

You Try to Keep Everybody Happy All the Time

Get over this now. You do not have the right or the power to *make* anyone happy or unhappy. Only they can do that. They can use you as an excuse for how they want to feel, but that does not mean you are the cause. At every moment every person is generating their own experience by virtue of the thoughts they think, the choices they make, and the interpretation they apply to events. An unhappy person will complain about a wisp of dust in a palace, while a happy person can make a palace out of a hovel.

> *It's not what happens to you that counts;*
> *it's what you make of what happens.*

You can keep happy those people who want to be happy, and you can't keep happy those who don't want to be happy. It's as simple as that. The notion of you keeping someone happy is a myth, a dysfunctional agreement, a social-sanctioned illusion. No matter what you do, people will find their own reasons to be ecstatic or miserable. You can tell people exactly what they need to hear to save them grief, and still they will make painful defeating choices. You can show people how to achieve their goals, but if they are not motivated, they will pay no attention. You can remove people from self-defeating situations, and the moment you turn your back, they will return to them. Then, when you finally throw up your hands and shout, "I give up!" they may take their life into their hands and step to their next rung of power. They had to do it in their way, in their time.

The only person you have the power to keep happy is yourself. Do that, and you will be an extremely positive force in the life of everyone you encounter. You will also know how to deal with them when they have a problem. You can model behavior for others, influence, encourage, and inspire, but you cannot choose for them. Glory Hallelujah! You are free!

You Feel Responsible to Take Away Any Pain You Encounter

I have a friend who worked as an administrator in a church. Her job included greeting visitors to the church office and making counseling appointments for the minister. By the end of her workday she was often depressed. "I have a hard time being around so many people who are hurting," she confessed. "I guess I'm just insensitive."

But she was not insensitive at all. She was *too* sensitive. Actually, too responsible. As a successful corporate executive, she had developed a skill for putting out administrative fires and getting jobs handled. When it came to working with people, she discovered that she could not put out their fires for them. Spreadsheets were one thing, human beings another. Her depression issued from her frustration in being unable to make things all right for everyone.

If you believe it is your job to lift pain from everyone who steps into your world, you will feel overwhelmed and depleted. You can offer love, kindness, caring, and relief, but in the end, others must make the choices that remove their pain.

There is a way to deal with people in pain that will really help them (and you): See beyond the pain. Hold the vision of the inner person, the one who is strong, capable, and empowered. Even while pain is in their face (and yours), they remain whole and intact. Pain can take away your client's peace, but not their potential. It may distress their body, but it cannot extinguish their spirit. All pain is fleeting and eventually gives way to well-being. On one day the person may be in the pits, and the next day on top of the world. If you can affirm the top-of-the-world person even while they are hurting, you are in the strongest position to restore their power quickly.

I am not suggesting that you deny their pain or make believe they are not upset. If you challenge their experience, you create resistance and undermine your effectiveness. Just gently know they are more. Know that they will come out on the other side and they have the tools to get there. Their challenge, difficult as it may loom in this moment, is propelling them to greater awareness and aliveness. They were strong enough to take on the lesson, and they will be strong enough to master it.

Insensitivity is a debit to service, but oversensitivity is equally damaging. If you bump up against people or situations that drain you, pull back your feelers a bit. Your energy loss means you are delving too deeply into a situation that doesn't belong to you. You are to be helpful from a distance.

It is not your job to take away all the pain you see. It is your job to stay out of pain or, when pain arises in your life or another's, extract the lesson and pivot to peace as quickly as possible. When you encounter people in the process of pivoting, lend them a hand where you can, then support them to master their challenge in their own way and time. You will be amazed at how well things work out when you establish yourself in higher vision and trust the process.

You Equate Worry with Love

Worry is not an expression of love. It is an expression of fear and mistrust. If you fully trusted in the wisdom and strength of your loved ones and the universe that enfolds them, you would never worry again.

When you worry about someone, you affirm their problem rather than the solution. You take the energy you could channel toward their success, and invest it in the continuance of their difficulty. Your intentions may be sincere, but your methodology is self-defeating. Worry is destructive to both you and the one you care about. If you really want to help, direct your thoughts, words, and actions toward their desired goal and then don't back-pedal.

After my mother underwent major surgery, for some unknown reason she was not recovering. I, the dutiful son, sat by her bedside day and night, worrying about her. I watched and waited for her to show signs of regaining her strength, but I saw little. As the hours and days went on, I became increasingly anxious.

Then, after a week of sitting in that sticky vinyl chair, I contracted a staph infection. I was knocked out of commission and had no choice but to go home and lay in bed myself. It took me a week to recover, during which I was unable to visit my mother in the hospital. When I finally got back to see her, she was up and around, doing far better than when I had sat at the foot of her bed doting on her. My fearful thoughts were not contributing to her healing; they were delaying it. My fretting generated a force field that impeded her recovery. The best thing I could have done for her—which ended up happening—was to get my anxious energy away from her. Then she had a doorway to heal—and she did.

Quite often when someone is about to pass away, they wait until the family leaves the room. The moment the relatives step out, the person splits. When the family returns, grandpa is gone. Grandpa wanted to leave, but the fearful thoughts of the kin tethered him like a psychic rope. When the family stepped out, the runway was clear for takeoff. If someone is ready and desirous of passing, you serve them best by giving them space to do so. Of course this is easier said than done, especially if your loved one is very dear to you. Yet consider their passing not an ending, but a portal to a great adventure in which they get to start over. Then you can celebrate with them rather than mourn for them (or yourself).

In our culture we romanticize worry. When your lover says, "I was so worried about you," you feel loved and cared for. But think about it for a moment: Would you rather have someone worry about you, or stand confident in the knowledge of your strength and ability? If you were a football quarterback running for a touchdown and your spouse was your cheerleader, would you rather have her stand on the sidelines and yell, "Oh my God, he might not make it!" or "Keep going, you've got it made!"?

The antidote for worry is faith. Faith offsets fear and opens the door for miracles. Your loved ones are much more likely to succeed when you acknowledge their power, especially when they cannot feel it themselves. A friend is someone who remembers your song and sings it to you when you have forgotten it. Be such a friend to others, and both of you will live beyond the phony limits of fear.

You Identify Yourself As a Savior

If you have been a mother, therapist, doctor, minister, or teacher for a long time, you may become so immersed in your role as a helper that you don't know who you are without it. This identity, while noble and meaningful, becomes an albatross when you need to be just a person.

In my early days as a counselor I thought I had to have an answer for every problem anyone brought to me. One day my housemate told me about a difficulty he was having with his girlfriend. Immediately I launched into my therapist mode and gave him some advice. He looked me in the eye and told me, "You know, Alan, you don't have to have an answer for everything I say." That was the perfect response for me to hear—immensely liberating! He was right. Since that time I have given up being Mr. Fix-It. Usually it works better to just be Mr. Friend.

You Label People

Most labels stuff people into positions smaller than they are. Yes, you can be designated by age, gender, ethnic origin, skin color, socio-economic status, and genetic propensities, but those attributes represent only a tiny portion of the totality of your being. Ultimately such categorizations distract us from who we really are.

William Parker was a psychiatrist who cared little for his patients' labels. One day a young woman walked into his office with a 4-inch-thick dossier of her records as a mental patient, with diagnoses up the wazoo. Dr. Parker didn't even open the folder; he tossed it into his trash can. He took a seat on the couch next to his patient and looked her in the eye. "So, Rosemary," he began. "Please tell me what hurts and how I can help you." This set the stage for a therapeutic process that honored Rosemary as a whole person. Within a few months of working with Dr. Parker in this context, Rosemary made more progress than she had in many years of therapy and institutionalization.

Bureaucracies understandably depend on labels, but diminish their service in the process. Doctors and psychologists cannot get paid from insurance companies unless they label you. Often your problem must be boiled down to a number. You are not Mary, but a manic-depressive or, more simply, a 317. If, instead of "317," a psychologist submitted the diagnosis, "Mary is a very sensitive young woman who is trying to make sense of the huge changes in her life," their request for reimbursement would be summarily denied. So you get to be a 317. Then you start thinking of yourself as a 317 and everyone who meets you applies everything they have ever heard about 317s to you. Then you *really* become a 317. This goes for cancer, AIDS, ADHD, herpes, and every other disease with widespread (and usually demeaning) associations. That's why you're often better off not paying a lot of attention to labels others have applied to you, and not broadcasting them to others. Then you stand a fighting chance to be something more.

If you try to fix someone you have labeled, you shoot yourself in the foot (along with them) before you even begin. Half of the healing process is getting free of our labels, so why go there in the first place? A good healer does not get too involved in labels, and recognizes the client's potential beyond their classification. Use labels if you must to play the worldly game, but don't be bound by them. Everyone is God wearing an earth-suit manufactured uniquely for them. See beyond the suit and you'll both have a better time.

You Are Trying to Save the World

Over the course of history, more pain and suffering have been inflicted by zealots attempting to impose their religious, political, and moral beliefs on others, than any other cause. More people have been killed in religious wars and inquisitions than any other conflict (except fights over the remote control). Those who claim God is on their side alone are indeed alone.

The propensity to proselytize springs not from divine inspiration, but emotional insecurity. God loves, allows, appreciates, and respects. Impotent self-esteem seeks converts. In his book *New Seeds of Contemplation*, Christian mystic Thomas Merton wrote, "One of the first things to learn if you want to be a contemplative is to mind your own business. Nothing is more suspicious, in a man who seems holy, than an impatient desire to reform other men."

One who has discovered truth does not demand that others agree. To the contrary, an enlightened being revels in variety and uniqueness. They realize there are many paths up the mountain, and if we are each true to our own path, we all meet at the summit. The goal of making everyone a member of the same religion or political ideology is an egotistical fantasy born of immature understanding. The closer an individual comes to God, the more compassion and appreciation they bring to their fellows, and the less need they have to control others' behavior and beliefs. A truly free spirit allows others to be truly free.

The campaign to proselytize is engineered by the reptile brain. It reverts to the primal herd instinct that shrieks, "The larger our herd, the more we safeguard our survival and the greater our power to defeat our enemies." The reptile brain defines strength by numbers, while the higher self finds its power in love. (In the movie *The Matrix*, a computer hacker discovers his true identity as a creative spiritual being in the midst of a fear-based world of illusion. His name is *Neo* [as in neo-cortex]. Neo represents the part of the brain that transcends limitation-driven consciousness.) True spirituality soars far beyond a tally of troops. If you want to find spiritual security, leave the numbers game to the bean counters. (A very successful minister told me, "*Never count the house.*") Focus not on how many bodies are sitting in your church, but on how much joy fills their hearts. Hitler influenced millions of people to follow him, but they were all pitifully soulless.

Of course, when you find a religion or path that improves your life, it's only natural to want to share it with others. Indeed this is a loving instinct. The key factor is not your desire to communicate your discovery, but *how* you do it. Do you have an investment in others following in your footsteps, or can you trust that if they adopt a different course, all is well for them and you? If they indicate they are not interested or that they have found another path that works for them, can you respect their inner wisdom, release them to their route of choice, and continue to enjoy your friendship? If you can, you are secure in yourself and your path. If you feel upset or generate discord, you have not yet plumbed the depth of the wisdom you have touched.

The source of the desire to convert others is the psychological defense mechanism of projection, which the subconscious mind uses to avoid facing things about yourself you would rather not look at. Projection takes what is happening inside you and throws it (like the voice of a hypnotist) outside you so it appears that it is happening where you look rather than where you are. ("*You spot it, you got it.*") Ultimately projection generates a great deal of pain and confusion, since you are attempting to crucify or save others not from their sins, but your own. While you adopt a goal of world salvation, it is really your own you seek. (*A Course in Miracles* asks, "Can the world be saved if you are not?") If you are not willing to face your own shadow, you will try to rid the world of the evil you project onto a person or group (like Hitler and the Jewish people) or to get everyone onto your bandwagon.

I met a dear man who had recently discovered *watsu*, a beautiful soothing form of nurturing massage in water. The fellow had been deeply moved by his experience. He told me, "My goal is for everyone in the world to receive a watsu treatment." His languaging struck me. If a world watsu experience is his goal, he is going to have a hard time. There is no way everyone in the world is going to have a watsu; the logistics of arranging six billion watsus are quite infeasible. Besides, not everyone *wants* a watsu. Not everyone *needs* a watsu. Although many would benefit, his dream was an impossible one and a setup that only kept him at a distance from fulfillment now.

What this fellow was really saying was, "This treatment makes me feel so good that I want to feel this good all the time." It was *his* world he wanted to upgrade, which he got confused with *the* world. His mind, using the tool of projection, translated his desire for inner peace into world watsu domination. Oops. My friend would make far more progress if he just forgot about getting all the nations of the world into the watsu tub with him and concentrated his energy on staying in an enlightened attitude himself. Then, if he wanted to share watsu, he would do it from a purer place—and enjoy the process a lot more. Achieving his goal would not depend on the actions of others; it would depend on him.

If finding a path has helped you and you are enthusiastic about it, you will become a walking advertisement for it and you will have no need to coerce people to do it. They will notice how bright you are shining and ask you, "What have you been doing?" Then you can tell them with authority. But remember that your words are the least element of your message. *You* are your message. You will turn more people on with your being than your advertising. Your being *is* your advertising.

I have a deep respect for 12-step programs (such as Alcoholics Anonymous), which are among the most effective life-changing modalities of our time. They elicit real and lasting results, and their membership numbers in many millions. One of the traditions of A.A. is, "Our public relations policy is based on attraction rather than promotion." They do not need to sell themselves or manipulate people to join; the quality of their service is so compelling that it automatically attracts those who can benefit by it. And they will come of their own choice. When you wake up one morning in a strange bed, covered with vomit and not remembering how you got there, something inside you screams, "This sucks—I need help!" Then you are ripe and you show up to A.A. with conviction and willingness. And you will receive the help you need.

Another reason for A.A.'s success is that it is not top-heavy; the organizational structure is very light, and the institution exists to serve the members rather than the members existing to serve the institution. People with egos do not run the show; the principles run the show. When you let universal principles run your show, it will be a hit.

Some religions place a heavy emphasis on proselytizing and require adherents to go out into the world and come home with converts. The goal to convert heathens can seem real and urgent in the midst of a mass agreement that this is the thing to do. But agreement does not necessarily constitute sanity or reality—especially in a cult. Just ask the members of Jonestown or Heaven's Gate. But you can't ask them. They are dead. The police found them all wearing the same tennis shoes.

If you believe that your job is to convert souls, remember that the most powerful way to convert a soul is to bring it joy— not as you decide it should be joyful, but as *it* chooses. If you can help someone find relief, release from fear, and the recognition of their wholeness, you have served them in the highest way. Threats of punishment, damnation, and burning in eternal hell usually do not fall into the category of relief and release. You cannot scare someone into well-being; you can only love them into it. Upon occasion when I have not pandered to someone's attempts to proselytize me, they have told me, "I will pray for your soul." "Thank you very much," I tell them. "I appreciate all prayers for my well-being." Yet I wonder if they would do better to pray for their own soul, that they might find happiness that is not conditional on me joining their group. It is not what you are being saved *from* that is significant; it is what you are being saved *for*.

Years ago I participated in a popular seminar from which I received a great deal of value. Toward the conclusion of the program the trainers placed more and more emphasis on enrolling new members. The energy around this instruction felt "off" to me, in contrast to the wisdom the training had inculcated. We were told that the way to tell if you had learned the lessons of the course was by the number of people you brought to the next seminar; if you had really mastered the teachings, you would bring lots of people back. I wanted to prove that I had gotten the lesson, so I went about calling my friends to invite them to the follow-up event. As I picked up the telephone to call my first guest, I recognized a feeling I had experienced only once before in my life—when I had been hypnotized. Suddenly I realized that I was not making these calls because I wanted to; I had been programmed to make these calls. I had been engineered to be a bring-home-the-bacon robot. Immediately I hung up the phone and ceased the enrolling process. Later on, when my friends asked me about the program, I extolled the value of the teachings and even recommended they attend, but I did not set out on a mission to enroll new members.

A sage once confessed to his students, "A wizard has cast a spell on me which has placed me in a most distressing dilemma: Half of my teachings represent the purest wisdom that will bring you total enlightenment if you put it into practice. The other half is pure bullshit that will ruin your life if you follow it. My predicament is that I don't know which half is true and which half is bullshit." So it is with many cult-like religions and organizations: the institution offers priceless jewels couched in sticky bullshit. You have to figure out which is which.

If you are the object of attempts by others to convert you, your lessons are different. You must speak your truth. You must set appropriate boundaries. And you must do so with love and grace. If you respond with anger or defensiveness, you invite more. I have a friend who quit a cult 20 years ago, and he is still receiving mail from them! If you can master the lesson of a compassionate "no, thank you," you have learned a great lesson indeed—and you will be free.

Occasionally members of various religious sects show up at my door seeking to convert me, debate, or hand out literature. I greet them with love, thank them for coming, and tell them I respect them for following their faith. I do not sit down with them for theological debate. If I am busy, I tell them so. Or we might spend a minute or two talking about the weather, my garden, or my dog. ("A diplomat meets on a point of agreement.") I briefly speak with my visitors about things we have in common that bring us joy. Then I wish them a wonderful day. As they depart, they feel they have had a positive interaction; someone has been kind to them and not slammed the door in their face. I feel good about our time together, too. I did not join their religion and they did not join mine. But we joined as people for a pleasant moment. I call that a win for everyone.

You Marry Someone with the Expectation They'll Change

It is said that a woman marries a man with the expectation he will change, while a man marries a woman with the expectation she will never change. Many people (of both genders) go into marriages and enter into business arrangements with the starry-eyed hope that they will reform the other person once they sign on the dotted line.

After many years of counseling women who married with their fingers crossed, I can tell you that playing Pygmalion doesn't work. When considering marriage, what you see is what you get. Dive in only if you are willing to be with this person just as they are. You can't imagine the number of women who have told me they were sure that with enough love, effort, and commitment, they could get their prospective mate to stop drinking, carousing, or working 14 hours a day—once they got past the altar. Yet often after the vows were made, the behavior only intensified.

Romance novels and movies create the illusion that once the wedding rings are in place, everything changes and life will be wonderful forever. Wouldn't you like a dollar for every movie you have seen that ends with the much-sought-after-wedding scene? (And two bucks for every movie in which the bedraggled boyfriend crashes his beloved's wedding and snatches her from the alter as she is about to marry the guy she doesn't really love? Sheesh!) In the movie of life, the wedding is not the end of the movie, but the beginning. It is not true that "if I can just get him or her to say 'I do,' everything will work out." A husband or wife is not a fish you catch and take home to bake. They are a living, breathing person with unique intentions and free will. You, your partner, and your relationship are works in progress, and you can make wonderful things of your life together if you are both willing. But you cannot impose willingness; it must be born in the heart.

A rocky relationship or engagement is a strong indicator of a rocky marriage to come. (Remember: *Struggle to get, struggle to keep.*) Of course you can grow, evolve, and stabilize, but before that can happen, something in one or both of you must shift. Do not plan on shifting your partner. You have the right and power only to shift yourself. Usually your required shift is to let your partner be who they are. Then you become a catalyst for your partner to change. But—read my lips—don't let your partner be who they are with the underlying agenda that they will change. Shift yourself because it feels better to love than demand.

You Try to Get Your Kids to Live the Life You Choose for Them

Because your children are "yours" from birth, you may be especially tempted—even believe it is your right and responsibility—to get them to live out your agenda. Yet these big souls in little bodies arrive with a very strong agenda of their own, and you serve them (and yourself) by helping them get in touch with their own purpose and live it. Sometimes their intention matches yours for them, and often it does not.

If you keep trying to force your child into the mold you have fixed for them, your life will suck and so will theirs. Remember that they are here to teach you as much as you are here to teach them. Probably more. You will learn about letting go and they will learn about standing in their truth.

Sometimes you can train a child to be what you want them to be, but then they will need therapy when they grow up and have to come to my workshops. I don't want their business. I would rather see them self-actualized. Set them on that course by rewarding them for being real rather than accommodating. Love them into their destiny. One day they will learn that to achieve their dreams they must honor their uniqueness. Support them to learn that lesson by modeling that behavior toward them. My parents rewarded me not for speaking my truth, but for saying what they wanted to hear. It wasn't until I was 35 years old that I discovered I would get farther in life by being honest than by being a chameleon. Adaptability is important, but not at the expense of authenticity. Your child must be able to say no when they need to. If you listen for where your child's "yes" lives, you will respect their "no"— and they will respect yours. Respecting your child is your strongest investment in your child respecting you.

See your child not as a blank slate upon which you must write, but a gift package you must unwrap. In that little body lives a genius; help them bring it forth. Success is more about expression than impression. Not everyone is meant to go to college or marry within the religion. The more you try to force, the more resistance you will encounter. The more you appreciate and allow, the more joy you will experience and the better your relationship will be.

Of course you want to instill good values in your child. Training, discipline, and boundary-setting are required. But let these lessons be the backdrop for launching their magnificence. Good habits are the platform upon which the gifts of uniqueness are developed. Once you've set up the gantry for the rocket ship, step back and enjoy the takeoff.

You Try to Turn Friendships into Downlines

Network or multi-level marketing is a brilliant concept. I have participated in a number of network marketing plans and enjoyed their benefits. It's a great way to share valuable products and services, help your friends, and earn income.

Watch out that you don't start to see your friends as downlines only. Remember they are people, they have free choice, and you are bringing them your information to help them. If you launch into a sermon, try to frighten them with dire statistics of the horrible things that will happen if they don't purchase your products, or torture them with manic persistence, they won't like it, you won't sell much, and your friendships will suck.

Imagine the following scenario: You are sitting at home one evening totally getting into *Wheel of Fortune*, admiring how well Vanna White is holding up after all those rotations. Suddenly the phone rings. You pick it up and a strange voice greets you, "Hello, Terry?"

"Yes?"

"It's me, Julius."

"Julius?"

"Julius Schlemmermeir."

"Julius *who?*"

"Julius Schlemmermeir! Buddy! Remember we went to *Big Benny's Boat Burger* training school together in the summer of our junior year? I was the guy who got kicked out because I kept getting grilled cheese caught in my braces and the manager thought it was unsightly for the customers."

"Oh yeah, I think I remember. How ya doin'?"

"I'm doing great, Terry—just great. I was just thinking about you, and I figured I'd give you a call."

"Well, that's nice, Julius. How'd you get my number? I moved from Blowing Rock 20 years ago."

"I know. My cousin is a private eye, and he does me a favor once in a while . . . Say, Terry, I just had the most fantastic experience and I want to share it with you."

"What was that?"

"Well, it really wouldn't do justice to tell you over the phone. What say we get together for a drink one day after work?"

"I don't know, Julius, since my double amputation I have a hard time getting around."

"Nah, come on, Terry! Why let a minor setback get you down? Live a little! Remember the motto at Big Bob's: *Come on in and eat or we'll both starve!"*

"Well, all right. Are you in town?"

"No, but I can be. I can get a flight into Anchorage on Tuesday afternoon."

"You're going to fly to Alaska just to see me?"

"Buddy! We go back!"

Tuesday afternoon you roll into *Big Benny's*, where Julius is waiting for you with a thick glossy imprinted three-ring binder on the table. For a moment you wonder if you really do know him after all. But he seems glad to see you and he helps you onto your chair. You check to see if Julius still has grilled cheese braces and, to your relief, you find he has graduated from them. His eyes, however, look sort of glazed over. Maybe it was the long flight. Or perhaps he's not used to the 70-below wind-chill factor of the long Alaskan January nights.

You down a couple of beers and try to find some things in common to talk about. Not much there. Then Julius brings the notebook front and center. "Well, Terry, here's the amazing thing that happened to me. I am so excited to tell you about it!"

"Sure, Julius. What is it?"

"Pre-paid mortuary services."

"Pre-paid mortuary services?"

"That's right, Terry. It's the hottest thing sweeping the nation since Tickle Me Elmo! *Everybody* I know is getting in on it—and making big bucks. One of my friends quit his job as the President of the United States—now he works out of his house—sits in the living room in his underwear and just watches the checks roll in. He went from a check for 58 cents his first month to $3 billion his second month—and that's just the beginning!"

"Really?"

"Really! I'm telling you, now is your big chance to get in on the ground floor—you'll be set for life!" Julius flashes a dubious smile. Why does he remind you of Jack Nicholson?

"You know, Julius, I think I saw an infomercial about this on TV one night, with that Vietnamese guy Won Woppa

Scam. Then I thought I saw him on the news a week later, being dragged into a police car, covering his head with his jacket. Wasn't that the guy?"

"Nah, nah, you must have him confused with somebody else."

"Well, maybe. So how does this program work, anyway?"

"Well, that's the neatest thing, Terry. You don't work for it—it works for you. You see, you just get your friends to order these designer caskets, and you get a residual for every one they buy. See right here, you can get the casket with the Calvin Klein emblem for the ladies, Izod for the golfers in your life, and even a picture of Liberace for those with, you know, alternative lifestyles. And right here, you can press a button that activates a computer chip to record your voice and thank your loved ones for coming to your wake as they file past your casket. Talk about user-friendly! And if your customers take delivery now, you get an extra 5 percent commission!"

"Why would someone want to take delivery of a coffin before they die? Don't you think that's a little morbid?"

"That's just the beauty of the thing, Terry. If they take delivery now, at no extra charge the manufacturer will install a waterbed in the casket! Totally environmentally friendly— why kill trees when you can sleep in the same bed for a night or eternity?"

"I don't know, Julius, it seems a bit out there. Besides, I'm planning on being cremated."

"No problem, Terry! We've thought of that too!" (Julius pages through several more plastic-encased photos.) "We even have designer urns! If you want, you can have your photo embossed now at no extra charge! Our graphic designers can even do a little airbrush if you'd like to firm up that chin or extend your hairline a bit. Hey, if you're gonna have people remember you, why not remember the best? I tell you, these guys have thought of everything!"

"And I suppose if I take delivery now, it doubles as a karaoke machine?"

"Ha! That's a good one, Terry! I can see you'd make a fantastic network marketer! But you're not far off. Look right here at the urn from the top view. Can you see those little compartments inside?"

"Uh, sort of."

"Convenient storage for the mobile professional: Compartments for your cell phone, Palm Pilot, and laptop battery. All wired from the bottom of the urn for overnight charging. Plus, if you sign up now, I'll throw in estate-planning software. My friend, you can't afford *not* to get in on this. Do you believe you are worth it?"

Sound familiar to you? It's one way people mess up friendships. By contrast, I have bought network marketing products from people whose enthusiasm was utterly compelling. I never felt they were trying to force anything on me; instead, they were so happy to have discovered something that worked so well for them that they wanted to pass it along to the people they loved. Remember that your greatest sales tool is your energy. Your words and techniques are quite secondary. Believe in what you are doing; trust that the Law of Attraction will hook you up with the people you can best benefit; speak from your heart; trust your clients' wisdom to make the right choices, and you are good to go.

I know of a famous minister who has motivated many people to find happier and healthier lives. When someone asked him, "What is the secret of your success?" he answered, "I just set myself on fire and people watch me burn." Rather than taking a torch to your spouse, children, friends, or clients, turn up your flame. The joy you will experience as you let them be who they are will be so exhilarating that you will wonder why you ever wanted to alter them. Then you won't have to drag them anywhere; you will just enjoy them walking beside you.

YOU STARVE YOUR
Soul

From the moment Jerry saw Cathy, he loved her. She was everything he had ever wanted in a woman, and so much more. Cathy was so stunning, in fact, that Jerry got tongue-tied around her: his knees went wobbly and his brain imploded to mush. More than anything, he wanted to ask her for a date, but his sense of not-good-enough held him back. If he asked her out and she turned him down, he would be devastated. So Jerry simply became friends with Cathy; he would call her on the phone from time to time, and they would pal around at social functions. It wasn't what Jerry really wanted, but this relationship felt safe; he could be in the company of the woman of his dreams and not have to deal with the pressures of starting a relationship that might lead to pain and put her out of his life.

Finally, after months of dancing around, Jerry could stand it no longer. He got up the courage to tell Cathy he was interested in her, and he asked her for a date. When she accepted, Jerry was the happiest man on earth.

Quite self-conscious, Jerry showed up at Cathy's door at 7 o'clock on Friday night. She looked awesome! Cathy greeted Jerry with a hug and handed him a copy of one of her favorite books as a gift for him. He thanked her and escorted Cathy to his car, where he set the book in his glove box. Off they drove into Manhattan, where Jerry took his date to a Broadway play, then dinner.

But the evening did not go well—not because anything bad happened, but because Jerry was so nervous. Would she like him? Would they go out again? Could they possibly have a relationship? Could he please Cathy sexually? Jerry's anxiety prevented him from being fully present with Cathy or even enjoying her company. At the end of the evening the two said good-night and Jerry went home dejected. He knew that being so uptight must have made a poor impression on his date, and he had blown it. He felt so embarrassed that he decided not to call Cathy again. His fear had turned into a self-fulfilling prophecy.

Fast-forward ten years. Jerry never saw Cathy again; a year after their date he heard that she was getting married. Jerry is plodding his way through dating hell. He has had a few relationships, but none have measured up to his vision of what he might have had with Cathy. Then one day Jerry receives a telephone call from his old friend Hal. Hal soberly reports that Cathy has died at a young age. Brain cancer. The funeral will be Tuesday. Hal reminds Jerry that he still has a book Jerry loaned him years ago—the one Cathy gave him at the beginning of their date.

"Jerry, did you ever read the note inside the cover?" asks Hal.

"What note?"

"Cathy enclosed a note to you. It's been sitting inside this book ever since you gave it to me."

"I never opened the book," Jerry responds. "What's it say?"

"I think it might be kind of personal."

"That's okay, Hal, just go ahead and read it to me."

Hal opens it and reads, *"Jerry, it's tonight or never. Cathy."*

Amazing as this story sounds, it is true. Jerry never had his Cathy because he didn't think he was worth a woman of her caliber—but she did. Out of fear and insecurity, he denied himself what he wanted most. This story hits home because each of us has a Cathy—a vision of how wonderful our life could be; a delicious relationship; dream home; exciting career; deeply rewarding friendships; exotic travel; artistic expression; or sense of health and well-being. All of these powerful visions depend on one question: Are you willing to give them to yourself?

A friend asked me what I would do with 547,600 if I were given it as a gift. I immediately rattled off a list of things I would buy. Then he told me he was not referring to money; he meant the number of minutes in a year—far more precious commodities than dollars. We are careful about how we budget our finances, but give far less thought to how we spend our time—or even more important, how we spend our spirit during those minutes. Every moment is an opportunity to feed your soul. The quality of your life depends on how much you are willing to let life love you.

The main thing is to keep the main thing the main thing.

A Persian mystic proclaimed, "If I had two loaves of bread, I would sell one and buy some hyacinths for my soul." The care and feeding of your spirit is far more important than all your other efforts; everything else you do depends on it. When your soul is well-fed, you feel great; your health is radiant; you have energy and enthusiasm; your relationships bring you deep reward; and whatever you touch turns to success. If your soul is malnourished, nothing else works. You feel crummy; you get upset over all kinds of diddly stuff; you fight with people on a daily basis; your checkbook gets so screwed up that you have to close the account, open a new one, and hope that none of your old checks bounce; you spend most of your time at work putting out fires; and your love life is a horror show, epic drama, or disappearing act. Sure, you can put up a good front and fool a few people, but if you are hollow and aching inside, nothing you set out to do will bring you the satisfaction you seek.

Is-ness is your business.

When you recognize that your spirit is withering, stop and *do whatever it takes* to renew yourself. Get outdoors. Take your best friend to dinner at your favorite restaurant. Walk on the beach and drink in the magic moment when the sun kisses the ocean. Get a deep full-body massage with sensual aromatic oil. Rent your favorite movies, pop a huge vat of popcorn, and have your own film festival for a weekend. Plan or take the vacation you've been putting off. Marvel at your shadow under the full moon. Anything you do to feel better will shift everything else you do. As Ally McBeal noted, "When I eat Jello I feel better. Don't ask me to reduce it to a science."

We usually think of starvation as a physical problem, while it runs deeper as a spiritual famine. We've all seen those heartbreaking photos of starving children in Africa, with bloated bellies and big sad eyes. Yet every day on our own streets we see people who are materially fed but soul-emaciated. We think little of it because we have come to accept soul-starvation as a way of life. You can have vast material wealth and be terribly hungry spiritually. And you can have meager rations, yet be soaring spiritually. Learning to feed your soul is one of the most important lessons of a lifetime.

HOW YOU STARVE YOUR SOUL AND WHAT YOU CAN DO

You Are Too Busy

I have thought about producing a bumper sticker: *Going nowhere faster will not get you somewhere.* You can make yourself so busy that you gain the whole world but lose your soul. You can do the math. If you are going crazy trying to do more things than you are able, stop and refresh yourself. Are you a human being or a human doing? Mahatma Gandhi declared, "There must be more to life than increasing its speed."

There are two kinds of *bus*yness: the kind that is empowering, and the kind that sucks. As you move through your day, does your energy increase, or do you end up feeling spent? When I am true to my joy, I feel more alive at the end of the day than when I began. There are other days when I feel wasted. It's not how much I did that makes the difference; it's how I felt as I went.

Busyness is not a net cast upon you by an overdemanding universe; it is a choice you make. You have more control than you realize over your level of busyness and the stress it engenders. Two factors determine how busy you are and whether you end up empowered or exhausted: 1) The activities you choose; and 2) Your mindset as you do them.

Deciding or agreeing to do something often ends up taking more time and energy than you anticipate; endeavors are rarely what they appear at first glance. So give yourself some breathing room. (An ancient proverb suggests, "Unless your living room is big enough for an elephant, don't make friends with an elephant trainer.") To do a project properly, there's stuff you have to do to get ready, and then stuff you have to do to follow up. (Sometimes the preparation and follow-up take more time than the project itself!) It's no joke when people say that remodeling or building projects end up costing twice as much and taking twice as long as you expect. This is not a bad thing; just don't be surprised when it turns out that way. Always leave yourself some wiggle time.

Your reward in a project is not just in how it turns out, but in the relationship you develop with it as you create it. When you take the time to really be with what you are doing, every moment becomes an opportunity to connect with yourself and your venture. Then the result of your work will bear your signature of love and bless those who receive it. During this era of mass-produced items, chain-store shopping, and fast-food scarfing, what a treasure is a handcrafted work! Make your life a handcrafted gift, and you will leave a legacy for the generations.

You can always do one thing less than you think you can.

Anyone can do lots of things in a flighty way, but a master takes the time and caring to do a few things well. Be such a master. Our astonishing high-speed technology has made our attention span so short that we do not have the patience to experience what we are doing or complete it impeccably. We are busy running to the next thing. Our society now runs on sound bytes. My telephone company gives me only four rings to answer a call before the phone call is automatically forwarded to voice mail. That's about 15 seconds. If I'm outside the house or stepping out of the shower, I have to sprint like a track star to catch it. A survey asked a group of people under age 25, "When you telephone a friend, how long do you wait for them to answer before you hang up?" The answer was, "two rings." Another survey asked couples, "What are the three words you speak to each other the most?" Before marriage, the most common answer was, "I love you." Married couples answered, "Where's the remote?"

If you start to feel frazzled, testy, or run-down, you have overstepped a crucial line. Most people have some physical symptom that signals them that they are starting to run down their batteries. A sore throat, headache, or hemorrhoid flare-up is the universe's way of alerting you that you are getting stressed. Instead of working harder or overriding the symptom with a drug, step back and regroup. Replenish your spirit and then you are good to go.

If you have to do things that keep you busy, you can remain joyful as you go. Remember to value energy before stuff and connection before manipulation. When you do things in a hurry, you miss the party and undermine what you are trying to accomplish. Your appointment book is a navigational tool, not a vice you clamp around your head and squeeze. You can get everything on your to-do list checked off, but if your soul is gasping for air, your efforts have been for naught. Instead of writing down what you want to do, write down *who you want to be and how you want to feel* as you do it. What you seek is more spiritual than material. Keep spirit first and you will succeed spiritually *and* materially.

Many people use busyness as a way to avoid feeling. They do not want to face the issues of their lives, so they generate an endless stream of appointments, errands, and projects to avoid being with themselves. They say they do not have time to deal with their pain because they are too busy, but the *very purpose* of being so busy is to not deal with the pain. They are not running around; they are running away, which just drives the pain deeper. Blaise Pascal observed, "All of man's problems stem from his inability to sit in a room quietly by himself."

As a culture, we are very much in denial about our addiction to busyness. Denial stands for "Don't Even Notice I Am Lying." We have many 12-step and other support groups to deal with our cultural addictions to drinking, drugs, sex, gambling, and debt; yet we do not have many 12-step groups for *workaholics* or *busyholics*, which number far more in the population than any other single group of addicts. Living at the end of your rope may be typical, but I assure you it is not natural. Yet we accept busyholicism as normal, even respectable. If you were to show up at work drunk every day, you would soon be confronted and either fired or encouraged to get help. But when you work 12 hours a day, whittle your personal life back to a hangnail, and have to paste Post-Its on your hotel room TV screen to remind you what city you are in, no one questions that. You scurry frantically across town, flooring the gas pedal at yellow lights, amped by intravenous Starbucks, driving with one hand, punching cell phone numbers with the other, and trying to keep the hot Styrofoam cup of triple espresso between your thighs from thwarting your future parenthood. You pride yourself on multitasking and feel like an underachiever if you're not spinning at least three plates at once, checking e-mail on line 1 while toggling between your boss on line 2 and your honey on the cell. Then someone knocks at the door and when you return you forgot who was on which line. But WAIT A MINUTE! (Huff, huff, puff, puff.) Does this really feel good? Is this really how you were born to live? If you did this for the rest of your life, how would you feel when you leave? Is it possible you could actually have a *life*?

I sat in on a magazine interview with Dr. Stephan Rechtschaffen, CEO of Omega Institute and author of *Timeshifting*. During the interview he suggested that we might be happier and more successful if we focus on one thing at a time. "But aren't you dangerously influencing people against multitasking?" the reporter asked. My God, I thought, we've come to a point where we have to defend being fully present!

The Chinese written character for the word "busy" is a combination of two other characters: "killing" and "heart." Heart disease, the foremost cause of death in our culture, is just what it says: the heart is not at ease. It is stressed. It is pressured.

It is being asked to do more than it is designed to do. Yet heart disease, like all disease, can be prevented or reversed by returning to ease. And what is ease, but living in harmony with your intentions?

Each day set aside some time to do something to feed your soul. Treat yourself according to the style to which you'd like to become accustomed. Rassle with your pooch or curl up with your cat. Make smoldering love in the middle of the afternoon. Buy that new high-definition flat screen TV you've been eying. Dance naked to your favorite CD. Whatever you do, don't settle for a life without luster; then you become just another zit on the complexion of life. When your heart feels full, you will have so much more clarity and presence that you will easily handle the things that are problems now.

> *Everything outside you depends*
> *on what is happening inside you.*

You Are Burnt Out

In my seminars I have worked intensively with many people in the helping professions, including doctors, nurses, teachers, ministers, psychologists, and social workers. The most pervasive problem I observe among this population is burnout. Most of them are fried. They spend so much time helping other people that they forget to help themselves. They become so embroiled in their clients' problems that they take them on as their own. They measure their success by the number of people they service or the income they generate, at the expense of their aliveness and the gifts that issue from it.

If you are not true to your passion, you turn into a lifeless, hollow-eyed automaton and you present your students, patients, or clients with a horrific model of self-annihilation. (If this doesn't sound attractive, don't try it at home.) I learned this lesson by depleting myself when I over-scheduled many seminars in different cities and spent more time in airplanes and sterile hotels than in my heart. By the time I arrived at my programs, I was a walking tape player. I went through the motions, said all the right things, smiled, shook hands, hugged, and gave a good presentation. There was only one problem: I was not there. Everyone else went home with a smile, while I was parched as driftwood. Yes, I was expanding my career, but in the process I was shrinking my soul. That sucked.

One night I arrived home from an intensive seminar tour and just lay in my bathtub. My head hurt. My back hurt. My butt hurt. An inner voice spoke: *"This can't be it."* No shit, Sherlock. It went on: "You can't be teaching people to find peace and joy when you are missing it yourself. Get your life force back, and then you will be in a position to teach from authority. In fact, don't do *anything* until you find your center again." Okay, okay.

I looked around at my peers teaching self-development, and many of them were fried too. One gave up his multi-million dollar church ministry and nationally syndicated TV show to raise emus. One developed a devastating gambling habit and publicly bragged about the women he fucked (his own language) in the back of taxicabs. Another cancelled a major lecture tour when she collapsed from exhaustion. These were people who had started out as teachers of peace, and good ones at that. They had passion and strong messages to share. But they built a treadmill and then could not keep up with it. Is there a message here? Like the size of a drive-in theater screen?

Former Beatle George Harrison owned a gorgeous estate near where I live. A friend of mine went to dinner there with George. I asked her, "Did he talk about his music?" "Not at all," she answered. "All he wants to do is garden." A few years later George participated in an online chat on AOL. He broke the record for the number of people online with him: over 300,000. The questions to which he responded most enthusiastically were not about The Beatles, but gardening. I'm sure many chatters were disappointed, but I fully understand.

When George and The Beatles were in the limelight, fans (the word is short for "fanatic") bestowed the group with fantastic amounts of power that no human being could gracefully field. After George rassled for years with nutty fans and frenzied financiers, he turned for solace from his guitar to gardenias. It all makes perfect sense. He summed it all up: "They used us as an excuse to go mad, and then they blamed it on us."

Many helping professionals suffer the consequences of playing God, or at least dealing with people who expect them to be God. In the process of saving other's lives and souls, many lose their own. Currently the average expected life span of an American physician is ten years less than the national average. Is there a clue here? Was Aristotle on to something when he advised, "Physician, heal thyself?" In a sense, we are all physicians. We are all in service to others, whether as a mother, waitress, or auto mechanic. The critical question is: Do you own your service or does your service own you? Does your vocation empower you, or do you feel like you are hauling a hundred-car freight train?

Any career short of electric creativity means you have compromised. If all you are receiving for your work is money, you are being grossly underpaid. Most people do not experience livelihood; they are more familiar with deadlihood. So it's time to move to a new 'hood. When you allow your passion to guide you to your right livelihood, you will be hard-pressed to call it "work." While the Wright brothers were developing the first airplane, one of them told a reporter, "We can't wait to get up in the morning!" People who have found their true calling report that they are having so much fun, they feel like they should be paying people to let them do it. Yet they are paid well for their services, and rightfully so. Their gifts go far beyond the obvious service they perform; they are teaching (by example) authentic self-expression, which cannot be translated into dollars.

You don't need to be a Wright brother to be able to look forward to your day. Just be you. Heed your natural instincts. Tell the truth about how your work feels. When something lights you up, pursue it. When something shuts you down, step back. The world will not fall apart if you take care of yourself before your clients. It will come together.

You Deny Your Passion

We have been taught that passion is the work of the devil, while it is the voice of God. Whoever fears the devil serves the devil. Passion is the universe's way to get you to 1) Be in your right place at the right time; 2) Fulfill your personal purpose; 3) Experience deep delight; 4) Receive abundant income or reward; and 5) Serve others in the process. Your passion is your guide to your next step and, in time, all the steps that follow. It is your connection to universal intelligence. If you want to unsuck your life, tell the truth about your passion and live from it.

Now here's the part where you say, "Whoa there, bucko—if I followed my passion, I'd wreck my marriage and abandon my kids and leave my job and hurt lots of people. And if everyone just followed their passion, they'd go around raping and pillaging and strangling their Cub Scouts. Dude, you're preaching chaos!"

Then I say, "There, the Puritans just got you again!" If you think that following passion leads to raping and pillaging and strangling, you don't know what passion is. You *need* this book. Keep reading.

In the film *Legally Blonde,* a ditzy yet lovable young L.A. lady named Elle fudges her way into law school to impress her boyfriend. There she gets involved in a murder case in which a young aerobic instructor is accused of killing her elder husband. While Elle's team of lawyers is trying to figure out if the defendant is guilty or innocent, she comes up with a brilliant theory: "This woman couldn't have done it. She works out every day. With all those endorphins rushing through her system, why would she want to kill anyone?"

Elle's postulate is more than a joke. People who feel good

have no desire to do things that hurt others. It's only when people are *disconnected* from their passion that they engage in antisocial behavior. If we really wanted to discourage crime, we would support people to participate in activities that bring them joy. Those who commit aberrant acts are not following their passion at all; they are following their fear, rage, desire for attention, impulse to hurt as they have been hurt, and voices far distant from joy. If they had been encouraged to express their passion in healthy ways, they would not need to lash out and harm others. I assure you that Charles Manson, Timothy McVeigh, and Osama bin Ladin were not guided by the spirit of joy. So let's not hang crime on passion; the greatest crime is to not respect passion. If you are true to your passion, you will not go around raping and pillaging. You will go around shining and inspiring others to do the same.

You Treat Your Body
Like an Unloved Pet

If the humane society could rescue people who abuse their bodies like they rescue abused pets, a lot of us would find ourselves in animal shelters. Some of us take better care of our pets than ourselves. I used to raise macaw parrots, whom I treated like valued children. Every morning and afternoon I would fix them meals on a special diet of fresh fruits, nuts, seeds, and vegetables. Guests at my house would watch with amazement as I spent time preparing healthy, tasty food for them. Then I would go to the freezer, yank out a gnarly frozen bachelor burrito, and pop it in the microwave for myself. What's up with that? I fed those little buggers better than I fed myself!

Your body requires but minimal maintenance to keep it happy and healthy. If you feed it decent fuel, rest it, keep it out of toxic environments, and move it about regularly, it will stay in good shape and perform trillions of complex microscopic tasks (like the Krebs Cycle, the only thing I remember from high school) without any conscious attention on your part. If ever there was proof of an intelligent and resourceful universe, the human body is it!

If you do not give your body minimal nurturing, garnished with love and respect, your health will suck and so will your life. It's hard to feel good when you don't feel good. You will grow grumpy and pick on people who don't really mean to bother you. ("Quit looking at me in that tone of voice!") If more people moved their bodies in fresh air daily, chose a dietary staple other than beer, threw their television over a cliff (except for *Oprah*), and got a good night's sleep, many of our societal ills would be resolved in short order.

If your body is not working as well as you would like, despair not. With even a little effort you can restore your health to well-being, and with ongoing kindness to yourself, you can feel really good. There are thousands of good books on health care, but I will save you the trouble, time, and expense of going through them. If you follow the simple suggestions below, you will feel good and your body will be your friend:

Eat Right

Choose foods as close to their original natural state as possible. Avoid heavily processed foods and junk full of chemicals, artificial stuff, and preservatives. Don't eat anything with ingredients that you can't pronounce. Get over sugar, caffeine, and alcohol habits—they are costing you more than you realize. Drink lots of water. Eat several smaller meals throughout the day rather than a few large meals. Eat your main meal when the sun is high, and a lighter dinner, not late at night. Actually sit down when you eat. Don't balance your checkbook, talk about your operation, or get divorced while you are eating. When possible, eat in a pleasant, relaxing atmosphere. Say a brief blessing, if only to yourself silently. Listen to your body's response to the foods you ingest. Notice what makes your body feel good and what makes it feel bad. Discover your own diet. There are 5,212 diet books on the shelves, they all work, and they all contradict each other. No single diet works for everyone. Experiment. The best diet for you is the one that makes you feel best.

Rest

Take the time to renew yourself as you go. Get enough sleep; it's holy. Take naps. Get massaged. Go home from work at five o'clock. Take mental health days. Take vacations. Go to retreats for recreation and renewal. When you start to feel overworked, frazzled, or fatigued, stop and recharge. Step outside and breathe deeply until you feel good. Walk away from your computer when it starts to turn into Freddie Kruger's face. Say no and stick to it. Get away from people who drag you down. Quit dragging yourself down with critical thoughts. Don't try to force projects and people. Be sensitive to cycles: surf on the crest of the wave and coast in the trough.

Move

Do things you enjoy that get your energy circulating. Walk, jog, swim, work out, shoot some hoops, get out onto the golf course, do yoga or tai chi, putter in your garden or workshop, or do anything that moves life force through you. (Pressing buttons on the remote control doesn't count!) Don't make a burden or religion of exercise; do it for fun. You don't have to be Arnold Schwarzenegger or have a six-pack to be in shape. Just move until you feel good. Get your heart pumping, breathe deeply, and sweat when you can. Even a few minutes of regular vigorous movement will clear your brain and keep your body toned.

Get Outside

The great outdoors is the great healer. Put yourself in an environment of natural beauty. Read Thoreau's *On Walden Pond*. Sunbathe. Pick a sport that keeps you outdoors. Immerse yourself in the ocean or a natural body of water. Let air and light caress your whole body. Bring the outdoors inside with living plants and flowers. Find a quiet place in the park. Watch the sunrise. Don't be afraid of a few raindrops. Get a dog who will walk you a few times a day.

Sex

Enjoy it.

Explore Holistic or Alternative Health Care

Develop a relationship with a health care practitioner you trust. Find someone who gives you their full attention, treats you like a whole person, and is more fascinated with health than disease. Western allopathic medicine is helpful in emergencies and acute cases. For prevention and ongoing health maintenance, acupuncture, homeopathy, naturopathy, shiatsu, herbology, and many other forms of healing arts have achieved successful results for thousands of years. You may not need surgery or lots of expensive drugs with potentially harmful side effects. Natural healing, combined with attitude upgrade and lifestyle improvement, can bring you gratifying results that last.

You Don't Play Enough

I saw a video of a gang of monkeys who had climbed a tree with a long vine hanging over a pond. One by one the primates slithered onto the vine, swung back and forth with glee, and then leaped into the pond, laughing hysterically. Then they splashed their way to shore and scurried back up the tree for another round. The "barrel of monkeys" concept is real! The only purpose of their raucous behavior was sheer delight.

Then I began to wonder when was the last time I had swung on a rope swing. It had been a while. Did the monkeys remember something I had forgotten? Like to play?

Play is as important as eating and sleeping, and as important as work. If you forget to have fun, everything you do becomes awfully serious and a burden. No one is a bigger drag (literally) than someone who takes their work too seriously. Bertrand Russell noted, "One of the symptoms of an approaching nervous breakdown is the belief that one's work is terribly important." But life is too important to be taken seriously. We are here more to enjoy ourselves than to get something heavy done. If you live with a light heart, you are accomplishing more than someone who believes we are here to plod through life, suffer, and fix what is broken.

Play is an attitude. It is not something you block off time to do (although that can help). Play is a context in which you hold your activities; a good player can find a way to play with anyone, anywhere. Watch children who meet each other at a playground or someone's back yard. Within moments they find a way to co-create a delightful adventure. No credit check, Meyers-Briggs Personality Analysis, or urine test required. Their business is fun. As Doug Larson observed, "If people concentrated on the really important things in life, there'd be a shortage of fishing poles."

One day when I went to visit a friend I found him laughing heartily with someone on the telephone. When he got off the phone I asked him, "Was that an old friend of yours?"

"No, it was the I.R.S."

"You know someone at the I.R.S?"

"No, I had to call them and I got some guy. I figure as long as I had to talk to them we might as well have some fun."

When I visited the Soviet Union with Dr. Patch Adams, he wore his outlandish clown outfit nearly everywhere and distributed red rubber noses all over Russia. One day Patch approached a very serious-looking army officer guarding Red Square, and Patch put a rubber nose on him. I thought for sure he was going to start a war! But after a few moments the guard smiled and broke into a laugh. Even more than the soldier wanted to be a tough guy, he wanted to laugh. (Believe me, he *needed* to laugh.) Patch replicated this scenario time and again, and never failed to lighten up his "victims." Patch's intention was pure joy, and he touched the place in each person that wanted to respond.

More sophisticated forms of play nurture our soul, as well. Music, theatre, poetry, dance, fine art, reading for entertainment, sports, and hobbies are good soul vitamins. In our work-obsessed society we take time to nourish our soul only if there is time left over when we are done working. But, as you may have noticed, you are never done working unless you choose to be done working. So I suggest you make it your business to play. The result, you will find, is that you will get a lot more done at work in a lot less time, and have a lot more fun doing it.

In our culture the care and feeding of the soul is a lost art. People in our society would do well to visit "less civilized" cultures that remember to keep spirit first. Ironically, people who value joy and minimize stress are in many ways more civilized. (When someone asked Mahatma Gandhi what he thought about Western civilization, he answered, "I think it would be a very good idea.") Perhaps this story sums up our predicament along with its solution:

> An American businessman stood at the pier of a small coastal Mexican village when a small boat with just one fisherman docked. Inside the boat were several large yellow fin tuna. The American complimented the Mexican on the quality of his fish and asked how long it took to catch them.
> The Mexican replied, "Only a little while."
> The American then asked, "Why don't you stay out longer and catch more fish?"
> The fisherman answered, "I have enough to support my family's immediate needs."
> The businessman then asked, "But what do you do with the rest of your time?"
> The fisherman answered, "I sleep late, fish a little,

play with my children, take siesta with my wife, stroll into the village each evening where I sip wine and play guitar with my amigos. I have a full and busy life, señor."

The American scoffed, *"I am a Harvard M.B.A. and I can help you. You should spend more time fishing, and with the income buy a bigger boat. With the proceeds from the bigger boat you could buy several boats, and eventually you would own a fleet of fishing boats. Instead of selling your catch to a middleman, you could sell directly to the processor and eventually open your own cannery. You would control the product, processing, and distribution. You would need to leave this small coastal fishing village and move to Mexico City, then L.A., and eventually New York City where you will run your expanding enterprise."*

The fisherman asked, *"But señor, how long will this all take?"*

The American replied, *"15–20 years."*

"But what then, señor?"

The American laughed and said, *"That's the best part! When the time is right you would announce an IPO and sell your company stock to the public and become very rich—you would make millions."*

"Millions, señor? Then what?"

"Then you would retire. Move to a small coastal fishing village where you would sleep late, fish a little, play with your kids, take siesta with your wife, stroll to the village in the evenings where you could sip wine and play your guitar with your amigos."

YOU FORGOT TO ENJOY THE *Ride*

When I moved to Hawaii I bought a stately home on a hilltop overlooking a lush tropical rain forest. This gorgeous property afforded a 360-degree view of sunrise over the ocean, the summit of the dormant 10,000-foot volcano Haleakala, and a resplendent valley with a singing waterfall. Warm ocean breezes massaged clusters of bamboo swaying gracefully above golden gingers wafting their intoxicating scent through the valley like a heady perfume. Paradise!

The house came with a rental unit I provided for a couple in exchange for caretaking. At the time, I was traveling a lot and I was always coming or going. I would return home from a trip, hustle to catch up with my business and property, and as soon as I caught my breath I was preparing for the next sortie. I was busy, busy, busy, and I took little time to relax or play.

179

One day as I was rushing somewhere, one of my caretakers invited me to stroll around the grounds with her and look at the flowers she had planted. A bit reluctantly I agreed. As we were walking, she turned to me and commented, "You know, Alan, you have this beautiful home, but you never take the time to enjoy it. We are your caretakers and we get more benefit out of being here than you do. Every day we stroll through the grounds and listen to the birds. We watch the clouds turn pink at sunset, sip tea, and savor the night-blooming jasmine. Why don't you take some time to do the same?"

Her observation stopped me in my tracks. She was right. I was so immersed in my doingness that I missed the whole point of living there. Although a banquet was set before me, I was preoccupied with running around and distracted from the immense beauty right before me. I seemed to be getting things done, but I was really going in circles. Meanwhile, my caretakers stayed home most of the time and they were soaring. Something was really wrong with this picture. I felt a bit like the prodigal son whose venture to the far country was so disappointing that he begged his father to let him come home and just eat what the pigs left over.

That day I decided to accept the gifts I had given myself. I began to take more time to notice and celebrate the feast before me. The more I appreciate the blessings I have, the more blessings I find. Now I lose track of time in my garden, drift to sleep under the symphony of tropical rain on the tin roof, and on clear summer nights sit on my porch and count shooting stars. I have now gotten to the point where I am enjoying my life as much as my caretakers enjoyed my life.

No place is worth going if you miss your life along the way. On Maui there is a famous road to the remote town of Hana. The Hana Highway winds for 33 miles along breathtaking cliffs overlooking a turquoise sea kissing black sand beaches; then through Eden-like primordial forests ribboned with gushing waterfalls at nearly every turn. If you take this trip you will negotiate over 600 curves in the road (many hairpin), and

51 one-lane bridges. The average speed along the two-and-a-half hour drive is 20 mph. The ride to Hana is one of my favorite in the world; it is a feast for the senses and an affirmation of grandeur.

Drivers on the Hana Highway exhibit two basic attitudes: 1) Get there as fast as you can; or 2) Enjoy the ride. Most of those enjoying the ride are tourists, while the impatient drivers are local folks. Many of the locals have become numb to the beauty and they just want to get where they are going. But even with a heavy foot they can't get there much faster, so they just create a bunch of stress for themselves. Meanwhile, the visitors are having a fabulous journey.

Have a fabulous journey. There is nowhere to get. Wherever you go, you will find yourself. Set your goals and strive to achieve them, but remember that the process is as important as the product. When you arrive at your destination—and you will—make sure you have taken your heart with you. If your happiness hinges on the one future day when *It* will happen, you will miss all the days until then. Why trade many days or years for one? You can have it all. You can get what you want—your chosen goal—and you can get what you *really* want—the pleasure of the adventure.

HOW YOU FORGET TO ENJOY THE RIDE AND WHAT YOU CAN DO

You Are so Involved with Planning for Tomorrow That You Miss Today

There are two types of planning: the kind you have to do, and the kind you use to avoid what you have to do. What you have to do is live true to yourself. Everything else just makes you crazy.

I know many people who are obsessive planners. Some of them function quite well in the corporate arena and capitalize on their talent for handling details. They are in their right place professionally. The problem is that when they want to turn their mind off, they can't. They have two operating speeds: "high" and "off." They go, go, go, do, do, do, push, push, push—and then crash.

When making a plan, ask yourself if you are motivated by fear or by joy; self-protection or self-expansion. *A Course in Miracles* tells us, "A healed mind does not plan." Certainly we must make plans. But not as many as you have been led to believe. After a certain point, plans do not enhance our flow—they impede it. When you are in your right mind, neurotic planning has no appeal. You do not need to create activity to avoid silence or uncomfortable situations. Instead, you could simply trust that inner peace is your greatest resource for intelligent decision-making. When you are relaxed and clear-minded, you have access to inner wisdom that knows exactly what to do in all situations.

If you are an obsessive planner, the greatest gift you could give yourself would be to take a retreat by yourself in a mountain cottage without a TV, phone, or e-mail. For the first day or two your mind would bounce off the walls, and then something really remarkable would happen: You would remember who you were before your life became a whirlwind. You would feel the firmness of the earth beneath your feet, hear the trees whisper to you, and savor the breeze caressing your cheeks like a long lost yet eternally devoted lover. The warm morning sun would stir you and living creatures would reveal themselves as your kin. Eventually you would fall in love with yourself and realize that you have been distracting yourself not from your problems, but your magnificence. Then you could return to your techno-toys and make good use of them. Not because you need them, but because you have found you.

The planning you have to do requires far less effort and energy than the planning you use to escape from your feelings.

If you were fully present today, tomorrow would take care of itself. You would meet everyone you need to meet at the right time, and wonderful synchronicities would occur. In Bali I stayed near a remote mountain village without easy access to telephones. On many occasions I wanted or needed to communicate with someone on the island, but had no way to get in touch with them. Then I would walk into the village, sit down at a sidewalk café, and sip some tea. A few minutes later the person I was trying to contact would show up. In tropical regions, this level of communication is called "the coconut wireless." It is real and it works!

Make whatever plans you need to make, then leave space for the universe to work its magic. If you keep your schedule full so nothing goes wrong, you may block the way for something better to go right. The gaps you leave will open doors for miracles. A friend once told me, "The best parts of my day are the interruptions." Make plans to fall back on, not fall into. You will discover there is a plan that runs far deeper than the ones you formulate, and it will provide for you impeccably.

You Live in the Past

Resisting the past is as much a distraction as resisting the future, and equally self-sabotaging. If you are uncomfortable here now, the past offers an attractive yet delusional escape. You might hide in history in one of three ways: 1) Romanticize it; 2) Regret it; or 3) Analyze it. Yet there are only two ways to relate to the past that will do you any good: 1) Appreciate it; and 2) Learn from it.

Romanticizing the past is seductive. It's fun to remember delightful experiences, but no fun to compare them to a present that doesn't measure up. I used to romanticize past relationships to the point where I believed I had missed out on being with my true soulmate. Then I would run into my former partner and remembered why we were not together. Or I would see the life path she had chosen and realize it did not match mine. It was right that we were together and right that we parted. So it is for all past experiences. They served you at the time and contributed to who and where you are today. But you cannot go back. The present moment is your cutting edge of aliveness and your true point of power.

If you regret the past, you overlook the gifts it has bestowed upon you. If you see yourself as a victim, you deny your role as a powerful creator. If you feel guilty and believe you should have done otherwise, you are being too hard on yourself. If you knew better, you would have done otherwise. You did the best you could with what you knew at the time. If everyone had to be a perfect parent before they had children, no more children would be born. You learn to be a parent by having children, and you learn to be yourself by having experiences. Give yourself some credit for the strides you have made rather than ruing the ones you missed.

Analyzing the past evicts you from your heart and imprisons you in your brain. Yes, it is important to learn from your victories and mistakes; just don't dwell on them. They are springboards to appropriate action now, not distractions from it. Retrospect is a good teacher, but a meanspirited roadhouse; visit it occasionally, but don't check in. Likewise, if you spend a lot of time looking in the rear view mirror, you will not see the road before you. If you need to learn lessons from your past deeds, they will emerge. Don't sweat trying to find them; if they are significant, they will find you.

When you are able to give thanks for everything that has happened, you are free. Any resistance to what was, only diminishes what is. "Come, for all things are now ready." Have a seat at the feast in your honor set before you now.

You are never going to figure it all out, so you might as well give up trying and enjoy yourself. For every answer you find, a new question will arise. The reasoning mind is never fully satisfied; it will keep seeking for things to dwell on like a car radio scanning for stations but never stopping on one. Eventually you will come back to where you started and wonder where you have been.

The mind makes a superb servant but a lousy master. If you filter your experience through your intellect, you will strain out a lot of good stuff. A Hindu aphorism calls the mind "the slayer of the real." You can dissect your experience into oblivion. Perhaps you have heard about the two psychologists walking down a hall, and they pass one of their colleagues. He bids them, "Good morning" and keeps walking. The two take a few more steps and then one psychologist turns to the other and says, "I wonder what he meant by that?"

You can wonder what things mean until you lose their meaning. A good therapy for many of us would be to take life at face value and just show up. Our educational system is heavily weighted on information and sorely lacking in inspiration. School, for the most part, does not teach students how to live, but how to please teachers; not how to create, but conform. Quite often more education occurs through students' social interactions than through the facts they hear in the classroom. Looking back on my high school experience, the most valuable class I took was typing. I learned a skill that ultimately contributed to my self-expression and vocation. Rote facts stimulate the mind, but leave the soul wanting. Skills go a longer way.

I propose that high school graduates should be required to wait one year before going on to college. During that time they could work, travel, or set sail on self-discovery adventures. Then when they enter college they would know more about who they are and make their educational and social choices from a richer base of experience. When I graduated from college I spent ten weeks hitchhiking through Europe. I grew up more during that summer than I did during all of my high school and college years. I had all my possessions stolen the first week I was there; met a seductress who beguiled me; attended London live theatre every evening; gazed with awe upon Michelangelo's statue of David; swam at a nude beach on the Greek island of Mykonos; had a run-in with a Nazi in Austria; climbed to the top of the Masada fortress in Israel; and met many wonderful friends with whom I stayed in touch for years. Some of the experiences were painful and some were ecstatic, yet all were valuable. I came home 20 pounds lighter and an utterly changed person. None of it had to do with book learning. My classroom was life.

Dr. Fritz Perls suggested to "lose your mind and come to your senses." A friend of mine was staying in a city hotel room with a tiny window that afforded her a view of only a brick wall across an alleyway. Just a little light entered her room, so each morning when she awoke she would listen to the radio for the weather report. One morning the report forecasted rain showers, so she stayed inside for a long time. When she finally went outside, she was amazed to find it was a beautiful sunny day! Listening to your mind without consulting your senses is like listening to the radio and never stepping into the day. Sometimes the mind offers an accurate appraisal of reality; often it does not. Our true knowing is not intellectual, but spiritual. Thoughts are not the only medium of guidance; feelings speak more deeply. Your inner sight (in-sight) will reveal to you vistas inaccessible to the intellect alone. A friend of mind reported, "Last year I took the most important step of my life, and it was only 18 inches: I moved from my head to my heart."

You Impale Yourself on Your Goalposts

At the end of an introductory surfing class I took, the teacher left us with a brilliant motto to remember: *"The best surfer is the one having the most fun."*

The same rule applies to the art of surfing through life. You have been taught that the most successful person is the one with the most money, sex appeal, prestige, power, skill, strength, or speed. But the most successful person is the one having the most fun.

> *The only true measure of success*
> *is happiness.*

While your goals are important, none are worth sacrificing your happiness. And what is happiness, but appreciating what you have now? People obsessed with goal achievement evaluate life by how things turn out. People committed to happiness evaluate life by the quality of their experience. While destinations are worthy, in the big picture they are simply an excuse to have a delicious journey.

While reading John Denver's autobiography *Take Me Home*, I felt saddened to read that he was divorced from his wife Annie, for whom he wrote his poetic hit, *Annie's Song* ("You fill up my senses like a night in the forest . . ."). I felt disappointed that the love and devotion John exuded in this inspiring song did not sustain a marriage or last a lifetime. Then I realized it didn't matter. The love was real and alive when he was moved to write the lyrics. *Annie's Song* captured that moment of powerful connection for which we all long, and bottled it for listeners to tap into and drink from. Even if John's experience lasted for one second, the song provides us entrée to passionate devotion that gives our lives richer meaning and purpose. Experiences are temporary, but the spirit that animates them lasts forever.

If you look back with remorse and devalue experiences because they did not last forever or bring you to where you wanted to end up, you miss the gift of the experience. A day is no less glorious because it gives way to night; a gorgeous dress no less ravishing because it one day becomes tattered; a glowing career no less contributory because you retire; a meal no less delicious because you grow hungry again; and a great romance no less stellar because a marriage ends. Rather then denying your shining moments because they yielded to the mundane, glorify them because they transcended mediocrity. Savor them as precious gifts that will forever warm your soul.

The ecstatic Persian poet Hafiz exclaimed, "It's all just a big love contest, and I never lose." He also declared, "All a sane man can ever think about is giving love." When your life revolves around just getting things done, your world grows gray and you lose sight of your Big-Picture purpose. In sports, the act of the ball going into the basket, cup, or end zone represents but a few moments of the contest; it's getting the ball into scoring position that makes the game interesting. When you remember you are here not just to win, but to play, you end up winning all the time rather than just at the end of the game.

Greek poet Constantine Cavafy has captured the profound relationship between destination and journey in his immortal poem, "Ithaka":

> As you set out for Ithaka
> Hope your road is a long one,
> Full of adventure, full of discovery.
> Laistrygonians, Cyclops, angry Poseidon—
> Don't be afraid of them:
> You'll never find things like that on your way
> As long as you keep your thoughts raised high,
> As long as a rare excitement
> Stirs your spirit and your body.
> Laistrygonians, Cyclops, wild Poseidon—

*You won't encounter them
Unless you bring them along inside your soul,
Unless your soul sets them up in front of you.*

*Hope your road is a long one.
May there be many summer mornings when,
With what pleasure, what joy,
You enter harbors you're seeing for the first time;
May you stop at Phoenician trading stations
To buy fine things,
Mother of pearl and coral, amber and ebony,
Sensual perfumes of every kind—
As many sensual perfumes as you can;
And may you visit many Egyptian cities
To learn and go on learning from those who know.*

*Keep Ithaka always in your mind.
Arriving there is what you're destined for.
But don't hurry the journey at all.
Better if it lasts for years,
So you're old by the time you reach the island,
Wealthy with all you've gained on the way,
Not expecting Ithaka to make you rich.*

*Ithaka gave you the marvelous journey.
Without her you wouldn't have set out.
She has nothing left to give you now.
And if you find her poor, Ithaka won't have fooled you.
Wise as you have become, so full of experience,
You'll have understood by then what these Ithakas mean.*

Money Runs Your Life

In a classic skit, comedian Jack Benny is accosted by a man who pokes a gun to his ribs and demands, "Your money or your life." Jack, ever the penny pincher, stands there for a while with his famous deadpan expression, trying to decide what to do. The longer he deliberates, the more the audience roars with laughter; what would be a no-brainer for most people is a dilemma for him.

Is your money worth more than your life? Or is it simply one avenue through which your good arrives and you pass it along? Money is not a goal to be pursued; it is the natural effect of being true to yourself. If you worship money for its own sake, your life with all of its riches will slip by. If, on the other hand, personal fulfillment is your goal, you will enjoy spiritual reward and the money will show up too.

If you are struggling with a decision, take money out of the equation. If money were not a factor, what would you do? I have counseled many people trying to decide whether or not to take a well-paying job they are not energetically drawn to. Usually they come to realize that taking the job would be a sellout and they would not be truly happy in it. I often hear from these people later that they found another job that also paid well, but which resonated with their soul. Money follows spirit, but spirit does not always follow money. If you live true to your talents and visions, abundance will flow naturally. Live so that the way you acquire money increases your life force rather than destroying it.

We have been programmed to overlay many emotional issues over money that obscure its reality as a simple fact of life and medium of exchange. Most people stress and fight over money more than they enjoy it. Consider this probably familiar scenario: You are having an enjoyable conversation with a friend (or relationship with a lover) when the subject of money between you comes up. Suddenly the energy shifts and you become emotionally contracted. Your mode of expression shifts from lightheartedness to self-protection. Many people enjoy dear friendships until they enter into a business or financial partnership; then one or both of them get their buttons pushed and they end up fighting, hating each other, and parting. This is tragic. Money is important, but relationship is more important.

Re-invent your relationship with money by reframing it as a vehicle for creative expression and mutual support. Instead of worrying about having less because you are spending it, celebrate your role in its circulation. You are helping yourself to get what you want and helping others to get what they want. Take the affirmation, *"Every dollar I spend enriches the economy and returns to me multiplied."* And it is so.

The more you celebrate moving your money,
the more joy you will experience and
the more money you will have.

You can and should have all the money you want and need. It is not spiritual to be poor. It is unspiritual to *think* poor. Money is a form of energy, and you have access to an unlimited amount. Just keep money in perspective. Like the mind, it is your servant, not master. If you miss a moment of life because you are caught up in money issues, you have missed one moment too much. Treat money as your friend, hold it lightly, and it will keep coming home.

Your Possessions Possess You

When I bought my first house, I had no idea what I was getting into. I thought you just buy the house, it is there, and you get to enjoy it forever. *Not.*

When you purchase a house, car, boat, furniture, computer, home entertainment system, or any item, you enter into a relationship with it. It requires attention, care, and maintenance.

Your investment stretches far beyond the price you initially paid. It's like seeing a cute puppy in a store or kitten on the street. If you take it home, it will require your love and attention far longer than your initial impulse. Do so only if you are willing and able to give it the nurturing it deserves.

You can spend most of your life (and energy) collecting and maintaining your possessions. (Remember comedian George Carlin's hilarious routine on "stuff?") If this is your idea of fun, then do it. But many people are owned by their stuff more than they own it. They hassle to get it, sweat to pay it off, spend a lot of time keeping it intact, worry about others marring it, fight over who gets it in the divorce or will, and resist its ultimate demise. Your stuff can drive you crazy! Like money, your relationship with your possessions depends entirely on your attitude; what you own is not good or bad of itself; it is what you make of it.

The blessing in having a possession you love is that you develop a relationship with it. I have learned to relate to my home not as a burden, but a dear companion. I keep it clean, repair it, and decorate it as I like, and it feels warm and welcoming. People who visit my home remark that they feel peaceful when they enter it. Your home is supposed to be a haven for self-nourishment. If it becomes an office or battlefield or you have to wear a hard hat when you enter the kitchen to protect yourself from the shaky tower of dishes in the sink, you might want to think again about what you are doing there. What would it take to make your home feel really good? You don't need a lot of money or fancy furniture for it to be a sacred personal space. I have walked into the humblest apartments with minimal furnishing and felt as if I was entering a royal palace. Not because of the grandeur of décor; because the residents created an energy that matched their taste and sense of comfort and self-nurturing.

Have all the stuff you want as long as you are enjoying it. If it starts to run your life, either get rid of it or get rid of your attachment to it. Most people who collect a lot of stuff get to the point where they just want to dump it and simplify their life. They would rather travel lightly and enjoy the ride than drag a cumbersome load. Take an inventory of all of your stuff and ask yourself which items uplift you and which weigh you down. Then let go of everything that doesn't make you feel good. You can't afford it. Then you will be left with what truly belongs to you and you will enjoy every moment with it.

Your Drive for Security
Makes You Insecure

If you are not secure now, you never will be. Security has nothing to do with insurance policies, alarm systems, or wedding vows. It is entirely about attitude. If you are secure in who you are, no outer event can remove your well-being. If you are insecure, any passing event, however wispy, can unravel your peace.

The paradox about gathering external forms of security is that the larger the fortress you build, the more insecure you feel. Amassing security is like trying to prove yourself; if you proceed from a faulty assumption—that you are vulnerable—everything you do based on that assumption will only magnify your sense of risk. The more protection you have, the more protection you need. If, on the other hand, you remember that you are already whole and you always have enough, everything you do will prove your assumption. If you know you are strong, nothing can break you; if you believe you are weak, nothing can protect you.

A couple who had been married for a short time attended one of my residential seminars. The wife was insecure and jealous of her husband's interactions with the other women in the group. To the rest of the group, it was obvious that this man loved his wife very much, he was dedicated to their marriage, and his connections with the women present were quite innocent. Yet his wife had deep-seeded trust issues with men and a history of perceived betrayal. During our group process, another participant suggested to her, "Wouldn't it be a shame if you finally found a man who was trustworthy and pushed him out of your life because you were afraid?" Yet the wife's sense of insecurity was so strong that she continued to mistrust and accuse him long after the program concluded. A year later they were divorced.

Although you are quite secure, your belief in insecurity can make you insecure. Illusions are as strong in their effects as the truth. You can manufacture experiences that would not come to you if you did not invest your energy in protecting yourself from them. No thing or person in the outer world has power over you unless you give it to them. No arsenal of defense can protect someone who lives in fear, and no arsenal is necessary for one who lives in light.

Insurance policies and alarm systems can be helpful; use them if you find them valuable. Just remember that your true source of security runs far deeper. Your real security lies in the wisdom and love inside you and in the unique gifts with which you have been imbued. Who you are is far greater than the roles you play in daily life. Your power rests not in worldly manipulation, but universal principles. Found your life on these principles, and you are literally invulnerable. You will be in your right place at the right time, you will magnetize situations that support you, and your health and happiness will spring forth naturally. Security is an inside job.

You Avoid Death at the Expense of Life

The purpose of life is *not* to arrive safely at death. It is to live so well that death or the fear of it cannot remove your joy. It is to have such a good time that you don't even notice death when it comes. You just close your eyes in one room and wake up in another.

We have heard so many fear-based pitches about what happens after death that we spend much of our life resisting it. Religious horror stories have not scared the hell out of us; they have scared hell into us. You can become so preoccupied with the afterlife that you miss the during life. If you have ever watched someone die a natural death, the experience can be very illuminating, even beautiful. I sat alone with my mother as she passed on. She took a breath in, breathed out, and did not breathe in again. The whole process seemed very natural and well-orchestrated, and I realized she was exercising a deep wisdom. The process was not horrible, but liberating. We all know how to do what we need to do when we need to do it, and death is no exception.

Of course we all want to live long, happy lives, and there is no reason to glorify death or go looking for it. We have a purpose here, and we shall fulfill it. We will not leave a day earlier or later than our purpose requires. During our life we need give death no more attention than to bless it as a natural evolution of our life cycle and use its reality to inspire us to spend our time on earth well.

Every great spiritual teaching has confirmed that death is not the end of life; it is simply a transition to another state of consciousness. The Twenty-Third Psalm affirms, "Though I walk through the valley of the shadow of death, I will fear no evil." The operative word here is "shadow." The appearance of death is but a momentary obstruction of the light. Although clouds may obscure our vision of the sun, the sun is still there. And while death seems to come between us and life, it does not; it simply takes us by the hand and leads us to another room in a great mansion. Where could you land but in the arms of God?

Death has power over you only if you fight it. You cannot worship death (by your fear of it) and enjoy a glorious life. Any belief of loss gives reality to the illusion of death and bestows a blood sacrifice at its dark altar. In truth, everything that leaves your life creates a space for something new to enter. And what has gone is recycled to show up in a new form and serve elsewhere. Loved ones who die do not go very far at all;

they are just on the other side of a curtain. They can communicate with you and you with them. You do not need to go to a séance to talk with your departed ones; simply get quiet and call them to mind and heart. Attune with their essence and you will feel them. After going through my grief over my mother's death, I reconnected with her in a most wonderful way. I often feel her with me and she does not seem gone. How could I miss someone who is still here?

I do not feel sorry for people who have died; I know they are in a good place. I feel sorry for people left behind. They mourn not for the deceased, but for themselves. Yet if they recognized that life is eternal and not limited to a physical body, their grief would give way to deep solace. Of course it is natural to feel sad when a loved one leaves, and it is not healthy to try to squash or deny feelings of grief. I once performed a memorial service for a family whose son had been killed in an accident. I asked the mother how she was feeling, and she told me she had just been too busy to feel much. But she was too busy *in order* to not feel much. Let yourself feel what you need to feel, then let the healing power of love lift you to freedom. Your beloved has set out on a great adventure.

You, too, are on a magnificent adventure. Where it ends up is not as important as where you are in it. If you are true to yourself as you go, you will arrive at a place that is true to you. Your destination is more meaningful for the route you choose to get there. You can take the well-traveled path or colorful side roads. In the end, the only thing that matters is that you follow your own path. In *The Teachings of Don Juan,* Yaqui Indian mentor Don Juan Matus taught raconteur Carlos Castaneda that there are just two paths of life: the path with heart and the path without heart. If you choose the path with heart, Don Juan explained, when you come to its end you will bless your life. If you follow the path without heart, when you come to the end you will curse what you have done.

At every moment you are choosing a path with or without heart. No one knows your path with heart better than you do. If you are true to your visions, dreams, and values, your life will shine. If you deny them, your life will suck. In the end, the power lies in your own hands.

ABOUT THE AUTHOR

ALAN H. COHEN is the author of 20 popular inspirational books, including the bestselling *The Dragon Doesn't Live Here Anymore* and the award-winning *A Deep Breath of Life*. Alan is a contributing writer for the *New York Times* #1 bestselling series *Chicken Soup for the Soul*. His books have been translated into 12 foreign languages.

Each month Alan's column, *From the Heart*, is published in 60 magazines internationally. His interviews and articles have been celebrated in *Unity*, *Science of Mind*, *New Woman*, *First for Women*, *Personal Transformation*, *New Realities*, *Human Potential*, and *Visions* magazines.

A frequent guest on radio and television, Alan has appeared on many national talk shows. His video presentations are regularly broadcast on the Wisdom Channel, and he is a faculty member at Omega Institute in New York. He also guides groups on excursions to sacred sites such as Machu Picchu, Bali, and Egypt. Alan resides in Maui, Hawaii, where he conducts retreats in life mastery.

For information on Alan Cohen's books, tapes, Hawaii retreats, journeys to sacred sites, online prosperity course, and seminars in your area, please contact:

www.alancohen.com
www.whyyourlifesucks.net
E-mail: admin@alancohen.com
Phone: (800) 568-3079
Fax: (808) 572-1023

or

ALAN COHEN PROGRAMS AND PUBLICATIONS
P.O. Box 835
Haiku, HI 96708

We hope you enjoyed this JODERE GROUP book.
If you would like to receive a free catalog featuring
additional Jodere Group books and products, or if you
would like information about the Jodere Group,
please contact:

JODERE
G R O U P

JODERE GROUP, INC.
P.O. Box 910147
San Diego, CA 92191-0147
(800) 569-1002

Please visit the JODERE GROUP Website at
www.jodere.com